MULTICULTURAL EDUCATION SERIES

James A. Banks, Series Editor

Understanding English Language Variation in U.S. Schools
ANNE H. CHARITY HUDLEY AND CHRISTINE MALLINSON

Latino Children Learning English: Steps in the Journey
GUADALUPE VALDÉS, SARAH CAPITELLI, AND LAURA ALVAREZ

Asians in the Ivory Tower: Dilemmas of Racial Inequality in American Higher Education
ROBERT T. TERANISHI

Our Worlds in Our Words: Exploring Race, Class, Gender, and Sexual Orientation in Multicultural Classrooms
MARY DILG

Culturally Responsive Teaching: Theory, Research, and Practice, SECOND EDITION
GENEVA GAY

Why Race and Culture Matter in Schools: Closing the Achievement Gap in America's Classrooms
TYRONE C. HOWARD

Diversity and Equity in Science Education: Research, Policy, and Practice
OKHEE LEE AND CORY A. BUXTON

Forbidden Language: English Learners and Restrictive Language Policies
PATRICIA GÁNDARA AND MEGAN HOPKINS, EDS.

The Light in Their Eyes: Creating Multicultural Learning Communities, 10TH ANNIVERSARY EDITION
SONIA NIETO

The Flat World and Education: How America's Commitment to Equity Will Determine Our Future
LINDA DARLING-HAMMOND

Teaching What *Really* Happened: How to Avoid the Tyranny of Textbooks and Get Students Excited About Doing History
JAMES W. LOEWEN

Diversity and the New Teacher: Learning from Experience in Urban Schools
CATHERINE CORNBLETH

Frogs into Princes: Writings on School Reform
LARRY CUBAN

Educating Citizens in a Multicultural Society, SECOND EDITION
JAMES A. BANKS

Culture, Literacy, and Learning: Taking Bloom in the Midst of the Whirlwind
CAROL D. LEE

Facing Accountability in Education: Democracy and Equity at Risk
CHRISTINE E. SLEETER, ED.

Talkin Black Talk: Language, Education, and Social Change
H. SAMY ALIM AND JOHN BAUGH, EDS.

Improving Access to Mathematics: Diversity and Equity in the Classroom
NA'ILAH SUAD NASIR AND PAUL COBB, EDS.

"To Remain an Indian": Lessons in Democracy from a Century of Native American Education
K. TSIANINA LOMAWAIMA AND TERESA L. MCCARTY

Education Research in the Public Interest: Social Justice, Action, and Policy
GLORIA LADSON-BILLINGS AND WILLIAM F. TATE, EDS.

Multicultural Strategies for Education and Social Change: Carriers of the Torch in the United States and South Africa
ARNETHA F. BALL

We Can't Teach What We Don't Know: White Teachers, Multiracial Schools, SECOND EDITION
GARY R. HOWARD

Un-Standardizing Curriculum: Multicultural Teaching in the Standards-Based Classroom
CHRISTINE E. SLEETER

Beyond the Big House: African American Educators on Teacher Education
GLORIA LADSON-BILLINGS

Teaching and Learning in Two Languages: Bilingualism and Schooling in the United States
EUGENE E. GARCÍA

(continued)

Multicultural Education Series, *continued*

Improving Multicultural Education: Lessons from the Intergroup Education Movement

Cherry A. McGee Banks

Education Programs for Improving Intergroup Relations: Theory, Research, and Practice

Walter G. Stephan and W. Paul Vogt, Eds.

Walking the Road: Race, Diversity, and Social Justice in Teacher Education

Marilyn Cochran-Smith

City Schools and the American Dream: Reclaiming the Promise of Public Education

Pedro A. Noguera

Thriving in the Multicultural Classroom: Principles and Practices for Effective Teaching

Mary Dilg

Educating Teachers for Diversity: Seeing with a Cultural Eye

Jacqueline Jordan Irvine

Teaching Democracy: Unity and Diversity in Public Life

Walter C. Parker

The Making—and Remaking—of a Multiculturalist

Carlos E. Cortés

Transforming the Multicultural Education of Teachers: Theory, Research, and Practice

Michael Vavrus

Learning to Teach for Social Justice

Linda Darling-Hammond, Jennifer French, and Silvia Paloma Garcia-Lopez, Eds.

Culture, Difference, and Power

Christine E. Sleeter

Learning and Not Learning English: Latino Students in American Schools

Guadalupe Valdés

The Children Are Watching: How the Media Teach About Diversity

Carlos E. Cortés

Race and Culture in the Classroom: Teaching and Learning Through Multicultural Education

Mary Dilg

Reducing Prejudice and Stereotyping in Schools

Walter Stephan

Multicultural Education, Transformative Knowledge, and Action: Historical and Contemporary Perspectives

James A. Banks, Ed.

Understanding English Language Variation in U.S. Schools

ANNE H. CHARITY HUDLEY
CHRISTINE MALLINSON

Foreword by William Labov
Afterword by Walt Wolfram

Teachers College, Columbia University
New York and London

Published by Teachers College Press, 1234 Amsterdam Avenue, New York, NY 10027

Library of Congress Cataloging-in-Publication Data

Charity Hudley, Anne H.
Understanding English language variation in U.S. schools / Anne H. Charity Hudley, Christine Mallinson ; foreword by William Labov ; afterword by Walt Wolfram.
p. cm. — (Multicultural education series)
Includes bibliographical references and index.
ISBN 978-0-8077-5148-0 (pbk : alk. paper) — ISBN 978-0-8077-5149-7 (cloth : alk. paper)
1. English language—Study and teaching. 2. English language—Variation. 3. Multicultural education—United States. I. Mallinson, Christine. II. Title.

LB1576.C4198 2011
427'.973—dc22

2010031536

ISBN: 978-0-8077-5148-0 (paper)
ISBN: 978-0-8077-5149-7 (cloth)

Printed on acid-free paper
Manufactured in the United States of America

18 17 16 15 14 13 12 11 8 7 6 5 4 3 2 1

Contents

Series Foreword

LANGUAGE IS an essential component of a student's culture and identity. The ways in which teachers and classmates respond to their home and community languages significantly influence how students respond to school and whether they perceive it as a culturally reinforcing or an alienating place. As Charity Hudley and Mallinson point out in this lucid, engaging, and heartfelt book, the right to speak one's native language or dialect is a basic human right. The United Nations Convention on the Rights of the Child (UNICEF, 1989) and the National Council of Teachers of English (NCTE) have affirmed this right. The NCTE (1974) position statement "affirm[s] the students' right to their own language—to the dialect that expresses their family and community identity, [and] the idiolect that expresses their unique personal identity."

It is much easier for institutions such as UNICEF and NCTE to issue position statements affirming students' rights to their own languages than it is for teachers and schools to implement policies and pedagogical practices that honor and respect the home and community languages of students who speak non-standard varieties of English or other languages. Today, as well as in the past, students who come to school speaking a nonstandard variety of English or another language are often marginalized and discriminated against within the school by teachers and other students. One of my Latino colleagues was given five whacks with a ping-pong paddle by the principal when he spoke Spanish in school in the 1950s (personal communication, March 13, 2010). During the same era, a Paiute child in Washington State described how she was forced to stand on a milking stool in a dark room in the cellar when she was caught speaking her native Paiute in school (as cited in Wise, 2010).

An acrimonious and polarizing national debate ensued after the Oakland School Board passed a resolution recognizing the legitimacy of African American Vernacular English (also called Ebonics) on December 18,

1996. The school board encouraged teachers to build upon Ebonics when teaching African American students the standard variety of English. The resolution was consistent with the research and recommendations of respected linguistics, such as Baratz and Shuy (1969), Labov (1972), and Shuy (1967). However, the bitter debate reflected the low status and widespread misconceptions about Ebonics within the schools and the public writ large. This welcomed and informative book will help readers develop a better understanding of the varieties of English in the United States. It also contains pedagogical insights and examples that will help teachers create democratic classrooms in which students who speak nonstandard varieties of English or other languages can experience recognition, equality, and identity confirmation (Gutmann, 2004).

This useful and incisive book will help educators deal effectively with the growing ethnic, cultural, and linguistic diversity within the United States and the schools. American classrooms are experiencing the largest influx of immigrant students since the beginning of the 20th century. About a million immigrants are making the United States their home each year (Martin & Midgley, 1999; Roberts, 2008). Between 1997 and 2006, 9,105,162 immigrants entered the United States (U.S. Department of Homeland Security, 2007). Only 15% came from European nations. Most came from nations in Asia, from Mexico, and from nations in Latin America, Central America, and the Caribbean (U.S. Department of Homeland Security, 2007). A large but undetermined number of undocumented immigrants also enter the United States each year. In 2007, *The New York Times* estimated that there were 12 million undocumented immigrants in the United States ("Immigration Sabotage," 2007). The influence of an increasingly ethnically diverse population on U.S. schools, colleges, and universities is and will continue to be enormous.

Schools in the United States are more diverse today than they have been since the early 1900s, when a multitude of immigrants entered the United States from southern, central, and eastern Europe. In the 34-year period between 1973 and 2007, the percentage of students of color in U.S. public schools increased from 22% to 55% (Dillon, 2006; National Center for Education Statistics, 2008c). If current trends continue, students of color will equal or exceed the percentage of White students in U.S. public schools within one or two decades. In the 2007–2008 school year, students of color exceeded the number of White students in 11 states: Arizona, California, Florida, Georgia, Hawaii, Louisiana, Maryland, Mississippi, Nevada, New Mexico, and Texas (National Center for Education Statistics, 2008a, 2008b).

Language and religious diversity is also increasing in the U.S. student population. English Language Learners (ELLs) are the fastest growing group of U.S. students (Suárez-Orozco & Suárez-Orozco, 2001). In 2000, about 20% of the school-age population spoke a language other than English at home (U.S. Census Bureau, 2003). The Progressive Policy Institute (2008) estimated that 50 million Americans (out of 300 million) spoke a language other than English at home in 2008. Harvard professor Diana L. Eck (2001) calls the United States the "most religiously diverse nation on earth" (p. 4). Islam is the fastest-growing religion in the United States, as well as in several European nations, such as France, the United Kingdom, and The Netherlands (Banks, 2009; Cesari, 2004). Most teachers are likely to have students from diverse ethnic, racial, linguistic, and religious groups in their classrooms during their careers. This is true in the United States, as well as in most other nations, as is amply documented in the *Routledge International Companion to Multicultural Education* (Banks, 2009).

The major purpose of the Multicultural Education Series is to provide educational practitioners, graduate students, scholars, and policymakers with an interrelated and comprehensive set of books that summarizes and analyzes important research, theory, and practice related to the education of ethnic, racial, cultural, and linguistic groups in the United States and the education of mainstream students about diversity. The dimensions of multicultural education, developed by Banks (2004) and described in the *Handbook of Research on Multicultural Education* (Banks & Banks, 2004), provide the conceptual framework for the development of the publications in the Series. They are *content integration, the knowledge construction process, prejudice reduction, an equity pedagogy,* and *an empowering school culture and social structure.*

The books in the Series provide research, theoretical, and practical knowledge about the behaviors and learning characteristics of students of color, language minority students, and low-income students. They also provide knowledge about ways to improve academic achievement and race relations in schools, colleges, and universities. Multicultural education is consequently as important for mainstream White students as it is for students of color. Multicultural education fosters the public good and the overarching goals of the nation.

When I was a graduate student at Michigan State University in the late 1960s, I was introduced to *bidialectic,* a term that was attributed to Raven I. McDavid (McDavid & Dil, 1980), who was a distinguished sociolinguist at the University of Chicago. Bidialectic describes the ability of individuals to gain proficiency in more than one variety of a language. As Charity Hudley and Mallinson indicate, English—like other languages—is made up of a number of varieties. The status of each variety reflects the social position and class of its speakers.

A significant message in this adept and practical book is that teachers can help students become effective bidialectics who learn school English while maintaining their home and community variety. A bidialectic approach to teaching Standard English is not only effective, it provides students with the opportunity to maintain their home and community languages, which is a basic human right that this book can help teachers to actualize in "identity safe" (Steele, 2010) and empowering classrooms and schools.

—James A. Banks

REFERENCES

Banks, J. A. (2004). Multicultural education: Historical development, dimensions, and practice. In J. A. Banks & C. A. M. Banks (Eds.), *Handbook of research on multicultural education* (2nd ed., pp. 3–29). San Francisco: Jossey-Bass.

Banks, J. A. (Ed.). (2009). *The Routledge international companion to multicultural education.* New York and London: Routledge.

Banks, J. A., & Banks, C. A. M. (Eds.). (2004). *Handbook of research on multicultural education* (2nd ed.). San Francisco: Jossey-Bass.

Baratz, J. C., & Shuy, R. W. (1969). *Teaching Black children to read.* Washington, DC: Center for Applied Linguistics.

Cesari, J. (2004). *When Islam and democracy meet: Muslims in Europe and the United States.* New York: Pelgrave Macmillan.

Dillon, S. (2006, August 27). In schools across U.S., the melting pot overflows. *New York Times,* pp. A7 & 16.

Eck, D. L. (2001). *A new religious America: How a "Christian country" has become the world's most religiously diverse nation.* New York: HarperSanFrancisco.

Gutmann, A. (2004). Unity and diversity in democratic multicultural education: Creative and destructive tensions. In J. A. Banks (Ed.), *Diversity and citizenship education: Global perspectives* (pp. 71–96). San Francisco: Jossey-Bass.

Immigration sabotage [Editorial]. (2007, June 4). *New York Times,* p. A22.

Labov, W. (1972). *Language in the inner city: Studies in the Black English vernacular.* Philadelphia: University of Pennsylvania Press.

McDavid, R. I., & Dil, A. S. (1980). *Varieties of American English: Essays.* Stanford: Stanford University Press.

Martin, P., & Midgley, E. (1999). Immigration to the United States. *Population Bulletin, 54*(2), pp. 1–44. Washington, DC: Population Reference Bureau.

National Center for Education Statistics. (2008a). *The condition of education 2008.* Washington, DC: U.S. Department of Education. Retrieved August 26, 2009, from http://nces.ed.gov/pubsearch/pubsinfo.asp?pubid=2008031

National Center for Education Statistics. (2008b). Public elementary/secondary school universe survey, 2007–2008. *Common Core of Data.* Retrieved January 20, 2010, from http://nces.ed.gov/ccd

National Center for Education Statistics. (2008c). State nonfiscal survey of public elementary/secondary education, 2007–2008. *Common Core of Data.* Retrieved January 20, 2010, from http://nces.ed.gov/ccd

National Council of Teachers of English. (1974). *NCTE position statement: Resolution on the students' right to their own language.* Retrieved May 22, 2010, from http://www.ncte.org/positions/statements/righttoownlanguage

Progressive Policy Institute. (2008). *50 million Americans speak languages other than English at home.* Retrieved September 2, 2008, from http://www.ppionline.org/ppi_ci.cfm?knlgAreaID=108&subsecID=900003&contentID=254619

Roberts, S. (2008, August 14). A generation away, minorities may become the majority in U.S. *New York Times,* pp. A1 & A18.

Shuy, R. W. (1967). *Discovering American dialects.* Champaign, IL: American Council of Teachers of English.

Steele, C. M. (2010). *Whistling Vivaldi and other clues to how stereotypes affect us.* New York: Norton.

Suárez-Orozco, C., & Suárez-Orozco, M. M. (2001). *Children of immigration.* Cambridge, MA: Harvard University Press.

UN Children's Fund (UNICEF). (1989, November 20). *United Nations Convention on the Rights of the Child.* Retrieved May 23, 2010, from http://www.unicef.org/crc/

U.S. Census Bureau. (2003, October). *Language use and English-speaking ability: 2000.* Retrieved September 2, 2008, from http://www.census.gov/prod/2003pubs/c2kbr-29.pdf

U.S. Department of Homeland Security. (2007). *Yearbook of immigration statistics, 2006.* Washington, DC: Office of Immigration Statistics, Author. Retrieved August 11, 2009, from http://www.dhs.gov/files/statistics/publications/yearbook.shtm

Wise, C. (2010, March 9). *Multicultural education and indigenous populations in the United States: Domestic aliens in their native land.* Unpublished paper prepared for partial fulfillment of the requirement for EDC&I 569, University of Washington, Seattle.

Foreword

THIS IS a book about language variation for those who have the most serious interest in the topic: teachers who are face-to-face with students whose language differences are front and center. The book is for teachers who ask, "Do these differences stand in the way of our students learning to read and write?" and, if so, "What do we do about it?"

Charity Hudley and Mallinson come to this topic with deep experience in the field and in the classroom. They unite two major traditions of linguistic research. Charity Hudley has engaged broadly in the study of urban African American English, starting in our reading program in Philadelphia, then pursuing her own research in Washington, Cleveland, and New Orleans before returning to the Richmond area. Mallinson comes from the long tradition of sociolinguistic research in the rural South, initiated by Professor Walt Wolfram in Appalachia and North Carolina, before she arrived in urban Baltimore. Unlike most linguists, Charity Hudley and Mallinson know their way about the classroom, and they know what teachers want to know. This book is the outcome of their program for teacher training, the product of their years of intimate contact with the teaching profession.

This book focuses on three kinds of English: standardized English and its relation to two nonstandard forms: African American English and Southern English. Why these two? First, our *Atlas of North American English* (Labov, Ash, & Boberg, 2006) shows that there are many regional dialects of English that are becoming increasingly different from one another and from standardized English, including the English of Eastern New England, Canada, the Great Lakes area, Pittsburgh, and the North Central States. These dialects are distinguished primarily by their sound patterns, and though these variations may complicate the task of reading and writing, they do not do so in a way comparable to the impact of African American English and Southern English. Second, these other regional varieties are not salient social issues in the classroom. Most of their differences from standardized English are well below the level of conscious awareness, and speakers of these dialects do not suffer the continual attacks on their sense of self-worth that are associated with the way they speak.

Southern English and African American English are both subject to caricature and misrepresentation in the public arena. The traditional view is that these forms of English are the result of the personal deficiencies of the speakers: that they are the products of laziness, carelessness, and ignorance. This book provides the powerful counterargument that these varieties are not the result of deficits in language learning capacity but are the product of a different set of rules with their own logic and internal consistency. The authors believe that their case will not be carried by rhetoric alone but by the steady dissemination of knowledge. They provide a wealth of information about these nonstandardized varieties, drawing on the most current research in linguistic and educational practice.

Linguistic description can be daunting, with its special vocabulary and mode of argumentation. Charity Hudley and Mallinson do a fine job of bridging the distance between grammar and its realization in the words of everyday speech. Since my own knowledge of Southern English is less extensive than my knowledge of other dialects, I profited by their discussion of many Southern features. Their description of multiple modals in Southern English is especially interesting, and I particularly like the discussion of rate of speech: They make it plain what is actually meant when people say that Southerners speak slower than Northerners. The treatment of Southern politeness strategies is enlightening, along with its relevance to the classroom situation. I also appreciated their calling to my attention the systematic use of Southern intensifiers like *plumb deaf* and *slam through*. The extensive treatment of African American English is equally rewarding, drawing on the authors' active roles in research on this variety.

Throughout this book, there is a regular alternation between description of language and the insightful application of this knowledge to the classroom. One never loses sight of the primary goal: to lead students to a mastery of reading and writing of standardized English. The sections on "Strategies for Educators" move the reader to the most pressing question that faces the classroom teacher: What do we do on Monday morning? I find here a wealth of ideas. You, as the user of this book, will be able to judge better than I how best to use them. I might cite one example that bears on my own work. In our tutorial program for struggling readers, we regularly use extracts from the lyrics of our students' favorite hip-hop artists, concentrating on verbal play with big words. Charity Hudley and Mallinson directed me to the advanced vocabulary of Mos Def, which I was not alert to. My thanks to the authors for bringing me up to date on this and many other points of interest!

In sum, this book is an invaluable voice among the chorus of those who speak about language in the classroom. I hope you will find it as useful as I do.

—William Labov
John and Margaret Fassitt Professor
of Linguistics and Director of the Linguistics
Laboratory, University of Pennsylvania

Preface

In this book, we promote a multicultural, multidisciplinary model of linguistic awareness that addresses pressing educational challenges related to English language variation and culture in the United States. We provide critical linguistic knowledge that helps educators accomplish four main goals: to teach all students how to communicate effectively in various social and academic situations; to distinguish language variations from errors when assessing students' listening, speaking, reading, and writing; to help students address common language-related challenges on standardized tests; and to appreciate the rich variety in students' cultural backgrounds, linguistic heritages, and personal identities.

Throughout this book, as other scholars within the Teachers College Press Multicultural Education Series have done, we uphold language standards and promote academic success for all students, while appreciating the varieties of English that many students speak. We believe that a solid understanding on the part of both students and educators of the language patterns that students bring with them into the classroom helps all students attain academic success. We therefore explain and advocate ways in which educators can adopt linguistically informed ways of teaching standardized English and understand how the structure and use of standardized English compare to the structure and use of nonstandardized varieties of English that students may use at home. As we strive to advance knowledge about and respect for linguistic and cultural diversity, we follow in the footsteps of those who have come before us in the multicultural education movement, working to ensure that all students in an increasingly diverse United States are educated in ways that enable them to achieve to their highest potential.

Acknowledgments

ABOVE ALL, we thank our families. Anne writes this book in honor of Cynthia and Renard Charity and in memory of Alfred and Sarah Charity and Leslie and Annie McClennon. Special thanks to Chris Hudley, Renée Charity Price and Mike and Carter Price; Renard Jr., Alicia, Madeleine, Emma, and Olivia Charity. Thanks also to the Hudley family, most of all Marie, Jay, and Tiffaney Hudley. Christine writes this book in memory of Karl and Anna Hoffmann and in honor of Jim and Carla Mallinson. Special thanks to Stephen Mallinson and Josh Birenbaum, who read drafts of this book and provided immeasurable support along the way.

We owe immense debts of gratitude to our mentors and teachers. First and foremost we thank William Labov and Walt Wolfram, who found a path, illuminated its way, and guided so many others like us to follow it. Without you, we would not be the scholars we are today. We also thank Carolyn Temple Adger, Connie Eble, Darion Griffin, Lee Perkins, John Shelton Reed, John Rickford, Hollis Scarborough, and Calvert Watkins. We are indebted to James A. Banks, editor of the Multicultural Education Series; to Brian Ellerbeck, Lyn Grossman, Nancy Power, and Beverly Rivero at Teachers College Press; to our manuscript reviewers; and to Melissa Hogarthy and Rita Turner for their excellent proofreading of the manuscript. We also thank Dana Dillehunt, who took Christine's photograph for this book.

Heartfelt thanks go to our colleagues Norma Day-Vines, Catherine Evans Davies, Laura Heymann, Lisa Reedich, Nancy Shelton, Sarah J. Shin, Susan Sonnenschein, and Kelly Whalon, who read entire drafts of our book; it is far better for having incorporated your and your students' suggestions. We also appreciate the insights and encouragement of many other scholars and friends, including Samy Alim, Maryam Bakht, Angela Banks, John Baugh, Bev Bickel, Phillip Carter, Becky Childs, Ioana Chitoran, Marcia Farr, Adia Garrett, Lisa Green, Monica Griffin, Kirk Hazen, Uri Horesh, Jenn Karnakis, Sonja Lanehart, Jason Loviglio, Terry Meier,

Marcyliena Morgan, Abena Osseo-Asare, Lynn Pelco, Jeffrey Reaser, Angela Rickford, Gillian Sankoff, John Singler, Ida Stockman, Kia Symonds, David Truscello, Meriel Baines Tulante, Bert Vaux, Maryanne Wolf, and Adrian Wurr.

We recognize the support of our colleagues at the College of William & Mary and the University of Maryland, Baltimore County (UMBC), most importantly our department chairs, Jack Martin, Elizabeth Barnes, and Jodi Crandall. We also thank colleagues at Dartmouth University, Harvard University, North Carolina State University, the University of North Carolina at Chapel Hill, and the University of Pennsylvania as well.

We were fortunate to have many in-service educators read drafts of our book manuscript, including Renée Charity Price, Linda Ryden, and Lee Quinn. We also thank the educators who attended our past Summer Workshops at Virginia Commonwealth University. We learned so much from these educators and benefited from hearing what they had to say.

Our students have also been a great resource. Rita Turner was an invaluable research assistant, as were Brittney Calloway, Mackenzie Fama, Brian Focarino, Hannah Askin Franz, Rachel Granata, Louise Lareau, Robert Staubs, and Kenay Sudler. Students Jeree Harris, Joe Hayes, Vered Nusinov, Laura Strickling, and Samanthe Tiver also read and commented on material in this book. We further acknowledge the students in Anne's 2005–2010 courses African American English, American Speech, Introduction to Community Studies, and Language Attitudes and those in Christine's 2008 and 2009 courses Language in Diverse Schools and Communities, The Human Voice in Social Contexts, and Language Variation and Education.

We have presented some material from this book at talks, conferences, and workshops, including the 2003 Society for the Scientific Study of Reading; the 2008 African-American Women's Language Conference at the University of Texas at San Antonio; the 2008 "Building Bridges" conference at UMBC; the 2008 Summer Dialect Teacher Project Workshop at the University of Massachusetts, Amherst; the 2009 Conference on Culture, Language and Social Practice at the University of Colorado at Boulder; and the 2009 National Research Council workshop on Language and Education. We also benefited from feedback from scholars and students at Coastal Carolina University, New York University, Northwestern University, Stanford University, Tufts University, The University of Texas at Arlington, Virginia Commonwealth University, Virginia Tech, and the University of Washington.

Parts of this book draw on material we have published elsewhere. We acknowledge Anne's chapters "Standardized Assessment of African-American Children: A Sociolinguistic Perspective" (Charity Hudley, 2009), and

"African American English" (Charity Hudley, 2008), as well as Christine's chapter "'The Way I Can Speak for Myself': The Social and Linguistic Context of Counseling Interviews with African American Adolescent Girls in Washington, DC" (Mallinson & Kendall, 2009). We also draw from our article "Communicating About Communication: Multidisciplinary Approaches to Educating Educators About Language Variation" (Mallinson & Charity Hudley, 2010) and from Anne's articles "Linguists as Agents for Social Change" (Charity, 2008b) and "African-American English: An Overview" (Charity, 2008a). Each opportunity helped us refine our work in ways that have benefited this book.

We also acknowledge funding sources that have supported us. Anne acknowledges the National Science Foundation for DRL-0115676, SES-0512005, and SES-0930522; the QEP Mellon Initiative at the College of William & Mary; and the College of William & Mary Community Studies Professorship. Anne's research has also been supported in part by a Ford Foundation Diversity Dissertation Fellowship, grant HD01994 from the National Institute of Child Health and Human Development to Haskins Laboratories, grant R215U990010 from the U.S. Department of Education Office of Educational Research and Improvement to the American Federation of Teachers, and grant H325T090009 from the U.S. Department of Education Office of Special Education Programs. Christine acknowledges the National Science Foundation for BCS-0236838, the UMBC Special Research Initiative Support and Summer Faculty Fellowship, and a course initiative grant from the UMBC Alex Brown Center for Entrepreneurship.

Our deepest thanks go to the individuals, organizations, and institutions we have mentioned and any we have inadvertently omitted. We are truly grateful for your support.

1

Valuable Voices

When author Toni Morrison gave a Nobel Lecture after accepting a Nobel Prize for Literature in 1993, she chose to focus on how language is essential to humanity. Language is an act with consequences: It can be handled, revered, put into service, looted, withheld, and even destroyed. "We die. That may be the meaning of life," Morrison said. "But we do language. That may be the measure of our lives" (Morrison, para. 21).

Language is a central component of both culture and the educational process. The language that students bring with them to educational settings significantly affects how they perform academically. Some students come to school already speaking the standardized variety of English that is valued and viewed as being the most correct in educational systems. Not surprisingly, these students are often more likely to succeed in school. Many other students come to school without already knowing the standardized variety, and as a result, they may be faced with linguistic hurdles every day.

Multicultural approaches to education support the essential concept that each student is unique, and that uniqueness is central to the development of every student, academically and socially. Given that language is integral to both culture and identity, an understanding of language variation and language diversity is critical to the multicultural education mission. All educators need knowledge and tools to understand their students' language differences and variations, address the language-related challenges they may face, and support their educational development and academic progress. Just as Howard (2006) related the idea that "we can't teach what we don't know," we believe information about language diversity and accompanying practical strategies are necessary to effectively work with linguistically diverse students.

Throughout this book, we include real-world pedagogical strategies that make the linguistic information we provide tangible for educators as well as students. In applying these strategies, educators will gain a greater appreciation of the cultural and linguistic awareness needed when working with diverse student populations, while educators and students alike will become more mindful of language variation. The techniques and information we provide in this book have a direct impact on some of the most crucial areas related to student success, including how to prepare students for standardized tests and improve their scores; how to enhance students' speaking, writing, and reading skills in ways that facilitate their academic advancement; and how to guide students to communicate effectively in ways that are valued within the educational system and beyond. As information about language variation and diversity is integrated across curricula, educators and students will be able to work together to build the spirit of multiculturalism, and all students will become better equipped to accomplish their educational goals for success.

LANGUAGE VARIATION

The last hundred years of linguistic research have demonstrated that language variation is a normal process. Because language is always changing, language differences naturally arise. These differences are not the same as language deficits, errors, mistakes, or confusions. Nonstandardized varieties of English are as rule-governed, patterned, and predictable in their linguistic structure as are standardized varieties of English. We explore standardized English in Chapter 2 and two nonstandardized varieties, Southern English and African American English, in Chapters 3 and 4.

Despite these linguistic realities, there is abundant evidence that people often hold opposite, negative attitudes about nonstandardized varieties of English. In experiments, research has found that listeners (of many diverse social backgrounds) consistently rank speakers of standardized English as being smarter and of a higher status than speakers of nonstandardized English dialects (Lippi-Green, 1997; Preston, 1998). Listeners also tend to associate positive personality traits and higher social status with the voices of standardized English speakers, and they tend to associate negative traits and lower social status with the voices of nonstandardized speakers. From this research, linguists have confirmed that people often draw conclusions about a speaker's intelligence, education, and other personal characteristics solely on the basis of how the speaker sounds, without much other evidence (Koch, Gross, & Kolts, 2001; Rodriguez, Cargile, & Rich, 2004; Tucker & Lambert, 1969).

Speakers of nonstandardized varieties of English have also been shown to score systematically lower on standardized assessments of verbal and mathematical ability than speakers of standardized varieties of English (Scarborough, Charity, & Griffin, 2003; Terry, Evangelou, & Smith, 2009). Research has shown that these systematic differences are not due to lower intelligence on the part of those who speak nonstandardized varieties of English but rather are the result of a range of social and economic factors. As we discuss in Chapter 5, linguistic factors related to test design and test preparation are often at the root of these differences in test scores for students who speak nonstandardized varieties of English.

The information provided throughout this book enables educators to work with students in linguistically informed ways. We reveal how linguistic knowledge can be integrated into methods for teaching all students to communicate effectively in a wide range of linguistic situations. We address the linguistic bases for many common challenges that students face on standardized tests, and we discuss how educators may appropriately distinguish nonstandardized English variants from what are otherwise student errors in speaking, oral reading, and writing.

We offer a poignant anecdote to illustrate how this book meets this critical need. In the fall of 2003, Anne gave a guest lecture at a large research university, during which she explained the differences between language variation and language errors. After the lecture, participants expressed dismay that educators are not given this linguistic knowledge earlier in their teacher preparation programs. One teacher, a 30-year veteran of a major public school system, said that for her entire career, she had marked common features of African American English as errors in her students' writing. She now realized, she said, that explaining those perceived errors with respect to language variation would have been a better approach—if she had known what those variants were. What she had interpreted as students' continual, careless errors were actually predictable language variants. Such issues of miscommunication and misinformation are the very ones we address in this book.

This book focuses on language, but it is neither a grammar book nor a book solely for language arts educators. Information about language diversity is critical for all educators. In science, technology, engineering, and math (STEM) classrooms, for example, language and communication are central. STEM educators see the need to help students become *T*-shaped: to have deep, "vertical" disciplinary knowledge and broad, "horizontal" knowledge about social relations, which includes the ability to dialogue with members of diverse groups (Ravesteijn, de Graaff, & Kroesen, 2006, p. 70). Fostering students' abilities to communicate well with others improves educator–student communication and student–peer communication at all levels, as well as colleague–peer communication in adult professional settings (Morgan, 2006).

Students do not leave their language patterns at the door when they engage in any educational activity, including receiving tutoring, practicing art and music skills, attending after-school programs, competing athletically, and communicating with administrators and school support personnel, as well as attending classes. Educators in all roles must thus be able to effectively communicate with linguistically and culturally diverse students and also help them communicate effectively in order to enable students to succeed to their best potential.

LANGUAGE, STUDENTS, AND MULTICULTURAL EDUCATION

Issues concerning language, student achievement, and student opportunity are critical to the multicultural education movement and to narrowing the achievement gap in the United States (Darling-Hammond, 2010). The achievement gap refers to the troubling finding that groups of historically underprivileged students, especially with respect to gender, regional background, racial or ethnic background, and social class, perform below other students on a number of educational measures (Vanneman, Hamilton, Anderson, & Rahman, 2009). Though the term *achievement gap* has long existed, the term *opportunity gap* has recently been introduced to shift the primary focus away from so-called underachieving individual students and schools toward the persistent, society-wide hurdles that limit the opportunities for academic success for students from cultural groups that have historically been excluded from or received only limited access to education (DeShano da Silva, Huguley, Kakli, & Rao, 2007). Another perspective is that achievement gaps "may be more accurately characterized as cultural gaps" between students, teachers, and the larger society (Ladson-Billings, 2009, p. ix).

The multicultural education movement began as educators and scholars adjusted to the cultural, social, and educational challenges facing the increasingly diverse students in their classrooms. As Banks and Banks (2004) explained:

> Multicultural education is a field of study and an emerging discipline whose major aim is to create equal education opportunities for students from diverse racial, ethnic, social-class, and cultural groups. One of its important goals is to help all students acquire the knowledge, attitudes, and skills needed to function effectively in a pluralistic democratic society and to interact, negotiate, and communicate with people from diverse groups to create a civic and moral community that works for the common good. (p. xi)

Gay (1994) also stated that multicultural education explicitly values diversity and supports culturally contextualized teaching. These factors, she contended, are crucial to providing educational opportunities for all students, as "disjunctures in how different students learn in their cultural communities and how they are expected to learn in school cause much time and attention to be devoted to resolving these conflicts instead of concentrating on academic tasks." In comparison, "culturally contextualized teaching [makes] the educational process more effective for ethnically diverse students" (p. 19).

According to the U.S. Census Bureau (2008), the student body of American public schools has expanded dramatically in size and in diversity. By the year 2023, more than 50% of children will belong to non-White racial or ethnic groups, and by the year 2050, these children will make up 62% of U.S. youth. In multicultural America, understanding and respecting "diversity in education, based on ethnicity, social class, language, non-Western national origins, economic status, cultures, and interests, is no longer a luxury or a matter of choice—it is a necessity for the survival of society" (Gay, 1994, p. 8).

To effectively work with students from diverse cultural and linguistic backgrounds, educators need preparation and knowledge as to how language and culture shape learning styles and behaviors. Erickson (2007) states that culture is a socially acquired system of meaning and that variation in culture is analogous to variation in language. Cultural differences are certainly often expressed through language; for example, consider actions and ideas as diverse as what counts as being funny in a given culture, how to express sadness, what people believe to be male- or female-sounding speech, and how speakers signal their membership in a social group or clique. Language is particularly important when we consider how students establish their identities in relation to school and academic achievement. Labov (1972) demonstrated how the social networks of boys in the Harlem neighborhood of New York City correlated with their use of African American English speech patterns and with their social and educational outlooks. Eckert (1989) found that students in a Detroit, Michigan, high school used specific linguistic features to present themselves as nerds, jocks, or punks. Presenting oneself as a serious and formal individual, as a casual and laid-back individual, or as a class clown are just some of the other identities that may be signaled by variation in a given speaker's language and personal style.

In this book, we address how educators can value the voices of all their students by respecting students' cultural backgrounds and personal styles and at the same time prepare them for environments that require the use of standardized styles of speaking and writing. Difficult tensions sometimes arise surrounding the desire to honor a student's cultural heritage and the desire for the student to *sound* educated. As educators ourselves, we share the important perspective from multicultural education that students' cultural legacies must be respected, and we also understand the reality that students' language use affects their educational and economic opportunities. We therefore provide evidence to assert that students fare better in life socially, academically, and professionally when they learn standardized English *and* when they are encouraged to continue developing their home language varieties, and we offer strategies throughout this book to help educators integrate this linguistic information into educational settings so that all students have equal opportunities to learn and grow.

We believe that only with an understanding of the principles and patterns of language variation can the multicultural education movement fully address why students who do not come to school already speaking standardized English often encounter disproportionate challenges in educational settings. In this regard, we join the multicultural education movement with sociolinguistics, which is the branch of linguistics that studies language as it is used in communities and societies. We continue the quest to educate all students, especially those from cultural groups that have historically been denied full access to education, as we investigate how knowledge about language variation can be marshaled to help address barriers to educational opportunity.

WHO WE ARE

Anne H. Charity Hudley grew up in Varina, Virginia, a rural area outside of Richmond. Anne learned the language varieties found in and around the places where she grew up, which is also where she resides today. Anne teaches at the College of William & Mary, a public university in Williamsburg, Virginia, where she is affiliated with the departments of English, linguistics, Africana studies, community studies, and women's studies. She is also the director of the Linguistics Laboratory and is the first William & Mary Professor of Community Studies. In graduate school she served as a site supervisor for the America Reads program and helped to establish the McNair Scholars Program at the University of Pennsylvania. She has served as a trustee of the Orchard House School, a middle school for girls in Richmond, Virginia, and she teaches several service-learning courses in which her students work closely with students who attend Williamsburg–James City County Public Schools. She also works on service-learning and diversity initiatives with her sister, Renée Charity

Price, who is the chair of the history department at St. Catherine's School in Richmond, Virginia, which Anne and Renée both attended.

Anne is from a multiracial background (African American, Native American, and White). Because most of her classmates at the private school she attended in Richmond were White, linguistic and cultural differences between Anne and her classmates were obvious early on. For Anne, growing up as an upper-class African American exposed to her the fact that race still matters, even when educational and economic differences have been mitigated.

Anne's family has always been very important to her, and her grandmothers were strong role models. Anne's paternal grandmother was raised working class, and although she was a top student at the Virginia Randolph School, segregation and financial resources limited her educational options, and she was not able to go to college. Nevertheless, Anne's grandmother made the best of what she had, even practicing with Anne the French vocabulary that she remembered from her high school days. In contrast, Anne's maternal grandmother held master's degrees in both English and history; she taught Anne to read by the age of 3 and had Anne reciting poetry and conversing on topics in African American history by the age of 8.

Anne left Virginia to attend Harvard, and after about a year or so she picked up some of the features of a New England accent and Northeastern way of speaking. Graduate school in Philadelphia also brought a more intimate knowledge of language as it is spoken in the inner cities of the Northeast. After her studies were over, Anne moved back to Virginia, and she quickly readopted the linguistic markers that are characteristic of her native variety of English.

Christine Mallinson grew up in the small town of Salisbury, North Carolina, and now resides in Baltimore, Maryland. Christine teaches at UMBC, a public university in Baltimore, Maryland. She teaches in the interdisciplinary Language, Literacy, and Culture Program and is also affiliated with the Gender and Women's Studies Program. Most of her students in the Language, Literacy, and Culture Program are current or former educators, and she teaches several service-learning courses that partner her students with K–12 teachers in Baltimore schools to develop lesson and project plans on topics related to language and culture. Christine also tutors weekly with the 3–7 Academy at Paul's Place, Inc., an after-school program focused on helping Baltimore high school students succeed in high school and beyond.

Christine grew up in a White, middle-class family, surrounded by many different languages and language varieties. Her parents, who were originally from New York and Pennsylvania, moved to North Carolina for college in the early 1970s and never left. They found the South to be a warm and hospitable place, and over the years they even picked up a few of its language patterns. Christine's maternal grandparents were from Germany; they came to New York City when they immigrated to the United States, then settled in upstate New York, where Christine's mother was raised. Later, they moved to North Carolina as well. At home, Christine's grandparents spoke a mixture of English and German, which Christine heard from the time she was born, and she learned to count in German almost as early as she learned to count in English.

Christine's father grew up in Lancaster, Pennsylvania, and her family often traveled there to visit relatives. Christine remembers being fascinated by the language patterns she heard there, turning over her relatives' pronunciations in her mind's ear. Her paternal grandmother and grandfather both had long careers in the military, and her paternal great-grandmother was a high school teacher who, in the early 1900s, attended Syracuse University's Teacher's College.

As a child growing up and attending school in the South, Christine found that her days were filled with the sounds of different language varieties, and she developed an accent that was never strong but was unmistakably Southern. Attending college at the University of North Carolina and graduate school at North Carolina State University sparked her further interest in Southern language and culture, especially in Appalachia. She now finds Baltimore, a city that has been called the northernmost Southern town and the southernmost Northern town, with its many cultural groups and rich history, to be a compelling and diverse linguistic scene as well.

We think we get along so well because we have so many personal and cultural similarities. We were both talkative children who spoke and read at an early age. We both grew up in extended families with grandparents in the house and close by. Even more coincidentally, we both have direct connections to the town of Salisbury, North Carolina, where Christine grew up and where Anne's paternal grandfather lived. Maybe this familial connection explains our similar cultural temperaments, which undoubtedly came from our North Carolina–influenced upbringings and from the legacies of our families.

Academically, we come from the two big schools of sociolinguistics. Anne studied at the University of Pennsylvania with Professor William Labov, a leader in research on language variation, and together they have published many papers and texts, including *Portals to Reading: Intensive Intervention*, a reading instruction guide that is sensitive to the linguistic and cultural specifics of African American students (Labov, Soto-Hinman, Dickson, Charity Hudley, & Thorsnes, 2010). Christine studied at North

Carolina State University with Professor Walt Wolfram, who also conducted pioneering studies of social and ethnic varieties, including Southern English, Ozark English, Appalachian English, Outer Banks English, African American English, Vietnamese English, and Puerto Rican English. While studying with Professor Wolfram, Christine conducted research around North Carolina and was involved in the production of two documentaries on language diversity, *Mountain Talk* and *Voices of North Carolina* (Hutcheson, 2004, 2005). In our academic positions, we follow their legacies by involving our students in outreach that brings information and understanding about language variation into the public sphere.

Our similar academic backgrounds and the influence of the African American and Southern cultures that are native to us are the basis of the shared standpoint that underlies our writing of this book. At the same time, our different cultural heritages and unique personal experiences have led us to become the people and scholars we are today. We hope readers ponder their own personal standpoints, linguistic heritages, and cultural backgrounds as they read this book, finding points of similarity as well as difference between our experiences and your own.

WHAT EDUCATORS WANT TO KNOW ABOUT LANGUAGE VARIATION

During our work and outreach, many educators have expressed a desire for more information on how to best educate students who come to school speaking nonstandardized varieties of English. We surveyed various educators and asked them what questions and concerns they had about language. Some educators wanted to know how language variation affects the ways that students perform academically, particularly in testing situations. Others were curious about how to address the use of nonstandardized English features in students' speech or writing. Educators were also concerned with whether to change their academic standards and expectations for students' oral and written assignments based on students' language differences or whether such modifications would be a disservice to students in terms of higher education and the job market. Finally, educators wanted to understand how to give students the support they need to learn standardized English.

We advocate that educators build on the language patterns that students bring with them to school, helping all students learn standardized English without diminishing their linguistic and cultural backgrounds. Throughout this book, we provide linguistic tools that educators can add to their multicultural tool kits that will help them become better equipped to teach standardized English to all students, while respecting students' diverse linguistic heritages and specific cultures. We respond to educators' questions and concerns about language variation in five chapters. Chapter 1, "Valuable Voices," has discussed the need for educators to know about language variation as a critical component of the multicultural education movement. The next four chapters provide more detailed information and practical strategies for educators. Chapter 2—"What Is Standard English?"—investigates English language standards as conceived in the U.S. educational system and in many educational and popular texts. Chapters 3 and 4 cover two of the most well-known and well-researched varieties of English in the United States: Southern English, a regional and cultural variety of English, and African American English, an ethnic and cultural variety. We explain what is unique about each variety and provide examples of its features. We offer practical pedagogical strategies that will help educators serve students who speak these nonstandardized varieties of English and work with *all* students to understand, appreciate, and benefit from knowledge about language variation. Chapter 5, "Assessment and Application," focuses on how knowledge of language variation is critical in the assessment of nonstandardized English–speaking students. We also explore further resources for educators seeking to promote linguistic awareness in their schools and communities.

A Web site also accompanies this book, available at http://charityhudleymallinson.com. We provide additional information about language and education and include sources for further reading as well as multimedia content that demonstrates structures and sounds of varieties of English. Thus, educators will be able to read about aspects of language variation in this book and then go online to hear examples of specific linguistic variants and recognize them in use.

2

What Is Standard English?

When teaching students about English usage, educators face many challenges. There is often limited time to provide sustained, significant, direct English instruction to students who need it most. Students who are already behind or who are not familiar with standardized reading, writing, and oral communication conventions are often those who come from nonstandardized English–speaking backgrounds. Such students may have a difficult time acquiring the voice and style that is valued in school. In this chapter, we discuss English language standards and the complexities of standardized English. We explore ways that educators can help all students learn the rules, norms, and conventions of the varieties of English they are expected to use in school and thereby meet language-related educational goals for school success.

ENGLISH LANGUAGE STANDARDS

Regardless of whether or not they are speakers of standardized English, most people have strong opinions on grammar, speech, reading, and writing. Conventions about the English language and language standards are often communicated in everyday conversation, popular opinion, and the media, as well as in grammar books. Terms commonly used to refer to a preferred style of English include *Standard English, formal English, School English,* and *academic English,* as well as *proper English, educated English, good English,* and *correct English.*

In Chapter 1, we used the term *standardized English,* in intentional contrast to the term *Standard English.* The term *Standard English* may suggest that some sort of single standard variety of English exists, irrespective of social norms, registers, or situational contexts. Language is a social behavior, however, and the ways that people communicate and use language are always situated within specific contexts and interactions. Different situations often yield different standardized forms of talk. There is no one standard variety of English, as language is always changing, and variation is inherent within all languages at all times.

We use the term *standardized English* in line with other scholars (Dunn & Lindblom, 2003; Richardson, 2003). The term *standardized English* makes the parallel that just as specific types of knowledge are valued on standardized tests, so, too, are specific types of language valued within the educational system. Using the term *standardized English* also reflects the important reality that powerful people and institutions, including the media, are involved in decisions about when and how to standardize English. Political, social, and cultural privilege has often determined which language varieties of English were deemed to be more prestigious, socially acceptable, or "standard" than others (Bonfiglio, 2002). As Romaine (1994) noted, standardization is not an inherent characteristic of language but rather an "acquired or deliberately and artificially imposed characteristic" (p. 84). In other words, there are no objective, empirical, linguistic reasons why a standardized variety of English should be thought of as being inherently better than any other variety of English, whether it be Shakespearean English, Brooklyn English, Texas English, Australian English, Singapore English, or South African English. If any language or language variety has a prestigious label, it is only because that type of language is spoken by socially, economically, and politically powerful people and is not due to any independent linguistic qualities.

TEACHING LANGUAGE STANDARDS

There is a general consensus in the United States that speaking and writing English in a standardized way will help people get ahead in education, in jobs, and in life. The style of English that grammar books advocate tends to be highly valued in our society. Grammar book–style English is often viewed as the target for how students should express themselves in school settings and how adults should express themselves in professional settings.

DISCUSSION: LANGUAGE AND ETIQUETTE

How does language relate to the standards we adhere to in different social situations? Here are a few reflection questions on social norms we may hold about etiquette and language.

Do you think correcting grammar and pronunciation is a question of *ethics*, *etiquette*, or neither? What aspects of English did your educators praise or correct in your speech and/or writing? Would you ever correct someone's grammar at work? What about your boss, a senior colleague, or a junior colleague? Would you ever correct the grammar of a relative, such as a parent, a sibling, a child, a younger relative, or an elderly relative? Would you ever correct someone's grammar in front of a group of other people, or only one-on-one? What about over e-mail, on the phone, or in person? Why or why not?

A common position holds that speakers should learn standardized, grammar book–style English because, particularly in environments such as school settings, everyone needs to be able to speak with clarity and uniformity. The idea is that if everyone speaks in a standardized way, English speakers will all have a better opportunity to understand each other; otherwise, communication would suffer. Convergence on one way of speaking is not the only method to improve communication, however. This book also has the goal of facilitating communication among speakers of various linguistic backgrounds. We provide information about standardized English as well as nonstandardized varieties of English, so that educators may most effectively communicate with, understand, and serve a range of linguistically and culturally diverse students.

Another argument maintains that because standardized English is the language of education, commerce, and social prowess in the United States, everyone should learn the standardized variety, and nonstandardized varieties should be used only in limited settings, such as at home. Part of the debate over this perspective centers on the question of where and how speakers should use nonstandardized varieties of English (Delpit & Dowdy, 2008), because the perspective that nonstandardized varieties of English should have limited use can sometimes put these speakers in a bind. People who speak nonstandardized varieties of English understand that their language and culture are central to their identity and personal history and that one's language and culture are not like a set of clothes that can be easily changed. Speakers who hear the message that the patterns of communicating they grew up with should have limited use may feel pressure and anxiety at the prospect of having to change meaningful aspects of their identity and potentially divorce themselves from their cultural heritage in order to succeed.

A multicultural, pro-diversity perspective, in comparison, explicitly states that the right to speak one's native language and language variety is a basic human right (Birch, 2005; see also Scott, Straker, & Katz,

2008). The multicultural perspective values diversity, and proponents believe that mainstream cultural assimilation is not achievable, required, or desirable for a harmonious society. Those who adopt this multicultural point of view encourage educators to actively approach instruction in ways that are mindful of diversity, including language diversity. From this perspective, educators recognize the value of educating students about language diversity in ways that honor all students' linguistic and cultural backgrounds while also teaching the rules, norms, and conventions of standardized English that students need to succeed in school and life.

In this book, we take a multiculturalist and pro-diversity approach to helping educators work with all students to meet English language standards. We advocate that academic standards be maintained by explicitly instructing students as to the language patterns, norms, and conventions of standardized English. We provide information for educators to help students to communicate effectively with respect to register, context, and audience. As Smitherman and Villanueva (2003) noted, effective literacy instruction equips students for real-world situations that require effective communication with diverse speakers of different languages and language varieties in a wide variety of linguistic situations.

We also uphold the importance of understanding the norms of both standardized and nonstandardized varieties of English, specifically how and when they may differ from each other and how these differences may affect student learning within educational settings. In linguistic terms, we might refer to this concept as "respect for the idiolect," since a person's idiolect is defined as his or her unique language or speech patterns. Just as some students have differences in learning styles that result in individualized learning plans, language may also vary from student to student. Attention to language diversity is therefore an integral part of fostering the academic and social development of every student, which is one of the primary goals of multicultural education.

LEARNING LANGUAGE STANDARDS

In the face of the vast amount of terminology and many prescriptions for correct ways of speaking, reading, and writing, educators are tasked with figuring out which English language conventions to teach and enforce with students and how best to do so. Yet no two books treat questions of language standards in the same way. Not surprisingly, the search for a single standard grammar has been historically elusive as well. Poplack, Van Herk, and Harvie (2002) surveyed grammar books from 1577 to 1898 and found immense variability in which topics were covered and which rules were taught. Lynch (2009) contends that the notion of a literary standard is an innovation of only the last 300 years. Lynch provides examples of nonstandardized writing in the canon of English literature, demonstrating that authors who penned these literary works often did not follow the same linguistic conventions that students learn today.

Messages from Grammar Texts

In the contemporary educational system, many methods have been proposed for how to improve students' reading, writing, and oral communication skills (see, e.g., Applebee & Langer, 2009; Langer, 2002; Whiteman, 1981). Grammar textbooks and style manuals also vary greatly in their methods and the material they cover. Some textbooks argue that students should aim for a single "Standard English" norm. The difficulty with this approach is that many textbooks take a *you know it when you see it* approach to defining standardized English. Often textbooks refer to "formal English" and "Standard English" without explaining these concepts and without addressing how these styles of English differ from "informal" or "non-Standard" English.

For example, the 2003 edition of Prentice Hall's "Silver Level" *Writing and Grammar* textbook, used in many eighth-grade classrooms, stated:

> Standard English can be either formal or informal. Formal English is appropriate for serious and academic purposes. Use informal English for casual writing, or when you want your writing to have a conversational tone. . . . When writing formal English, you should observe these conventions: Avoid contractions. Do not use slang. Follow standard English usage and grammar. Use a serious tone and sophisticated vocabulary. (p. 31)

Students reading this text may not know what Standard English looks like, and they may not be clear on how it can differ between formal and informal contexts. They may not know what counts as "academic purposes" compared to "casual writing." They may not understand whether it is possible to write an essay that is both casual and serious or both conversational and academic. Students might also wonder what, exactly, constitutes a "serious" tone and a "sophisticated" vocabulary.

Another difficulty faced by many texts that advocate the use of "Standard English" is how to refer to nonstandardized English features. Many students use nonstandardized features, and many nonstandardized features appear in famous novels, plays, and poetry. For this reason, it is impractical to avoid discussing nonstandardized English. Yet textbooks often do not present in-depth material on language variation. For example,

Prentice Hall's "Platinum Level" *Writing and Grammar* (Carroll, Wilson, & Forlini, 2001) paid brief attention to some typical language variants. On the subject of double negatives, the text asserted:

> At one time, it was correct to use several negative words in one sentence. It was correct, for example, to say, "Father *didn't* tell *nobody nothing*." Today, however, only one negative word is used to make the entire sentence negative. (p. 608)

The text goes on to provide three correct ways to restate the sentence, without discussion of the claim that English used to accept multiple negation but purportedly now does not. The passage also does not explain whether "correct" is intended to mean "adhering to the conventions of Standard English" or is instead meant to signify a value judgment against multiple negatives.

Most important, the text does not mention that in many speaking or writing situations, the use of multiple negatives is considered perfectly acceptable, appropriate, effective, and even desirable. In an impassioned political speech, multiple negatives might lend emphasis or intensity to a speaker's words. In creative writing, multiple negatives are often used to great stylistic effect. As we discuss in Chapters 3 and 4, many professionals, including lawyers, politicians, and salespeople, value the ability to converse with different people in culturally appropriate ways, which may entail using language variants that are familiar to the listeners who are being addressed. Without this critical information, students' ability to learn how to decide whether or not to use multiple negatives in different communicative situations is hindered.

In a similar vein, other textbooks apply the label "non-Standard" to certain English features but do not explain why. For example, in the textbook *Elements of Language: Introductory Course* (Odell, Vacca, Hobbs, & Irvin, 2001), Chapter 16, entitled Using Verbs Correctly, had a passage that stated: "One common error in forming the past or past participle of a regular verb is to leave off the -d or -ed ending." The text then went on to give two examples, one titled "nonstandard," which read, "Josh was suppose to meet us here," and one titled "Standard," which read, "Josh was supposed to meet us here" (p. 446). No explanation for the feature was given: The text did not clarify the reason for the label "nonstandard," nor did it explain why this type of variation occurs (as a result of consonant cluster reduction, which we discuss later in this book). The passage also omitted a discussion of how educators can successfully explain the difference between the two forms to their students. Even though they see that students frequently use these and other nonstandardized forms in their speech and writing, educators still may remain unaware of how to acknowledge language variation in ways that also help students learn the conventions of standardized English.

Textbook discussions of language variation, when they occur, sometimes contain inaccuracies that may affect understanding. Often, information about language variation appears in the margins of the teacher edition pages, and full explanations for linguistic material are not available. For example, the *Elements of Language: Introductory Course* (Odell et al., 2001) included a note to educators that stated:

> Most of the nonstandard usage studied in this chapter appears in various regional dialects. These nonstandard forms are used in such spoken sentences as "Have a apple," "She don't like spinach," and "You did good." Tell your students that standard English is the language of business, government, schools, and colleges. To succeed in any of these settings, it is essential to be fluent in standard English. (p. 523)

It certainly is important for books to point out that many nonstandardized forms appear in the speech and writing of students who speak regional varieties of English. Regional language variation is one of the ways in which a framework for differences in students' language patterns is built. Yet the text omits the fact that language can also vary due to factors like family heritage, racial or ethnic background, personality, age, and social class. In addition, the words and phrases cited in this passage are not strictly regional language patterns. Sentences such as "Have a apple," "She don't like spinach," and "You did good" are found in numerous varieties of English, not just regional ones. Without accurate and detailed knowledge about what language variants are likely to occur in students' speech and writing, educators are left with few tools to explain and work with the variations their students produce.

Advanced textbooks tend to provide more social context regarding language for both educators and students than more elementary editions do. For example, the *Elements of Language: Fifth Course* (Odell, Vacca, & Hobbs, 2007) mentioned flexibility regarding *who* and *whom*. In Chapter 19, Using Pronouns Correctly, a Style Tip was provided for students:

> In informal English, the use of *whom* is gradually disappearing. In informal situations, it is acceptable to begin a question with *who* regardless of whether the nominative or objective form is grammatically correct. In formal speaking and writing, though, it is still important to distinguish between *who* and *whom*. (p. 619)

The text further drew students' attention to the concept of *register*, or the different communication situations that call for different uses of language.

The *Elements of Language: Fifth Course* (Odell et al., 2007) also discussed flexible use of language in a brief passage on slang in Chapter 22. A tip labeled Inclusion gave this advice to educators:

> Remind students that some instances of informal usage or slang that are appropriate within their peer group, or in writing dialogue, are inappropriate in formal writing and speaking. For example, the slang terms *bad* and *baddest* mean *good* and *best*. Ask the class to discuss the use of *bad* and to give examples of how they use it. Point out to students that it is important to be fluent in both informal and formal English. (p. 697)

The text indicated that in many social situations, such as with peer groups or in writing dialogue, speaking too formally may be inappropriate. It also went on to assert that it is important for students to know how to use formal *and* informal English.

The end of the *Elements of Language: Fifth Course* (Odell et al., 2007) had a Quick Reference section, which included a "History of English" containing entries on language variation and Standard English. Under the heading Dialects of American English, the text read, "Everyone uses a dialect, and no dialect is better or worse than another. . . . *Ethnic dialects* are the speech patterns of special communities that have preserved some of their heritage from the past" (p. 939). The Fifth Course went on to describe and give a brief historical context for "one of the most prominent ethnic dialects in the United States," the "African American dialect." The text gave three examples of features of African American English: "*aunt* pronounced 'ahnt,' *He be sick* meaning a 'continuing rather than temporary illness,' and *tote* meaning 'carry'" (p. 939). Hispanic English was also mentioned. This section provided examples of the grammar and vocabulary of select regional varieties as well.

The Fifth Course also included a section titled Standard English. In this carefully elaborated definition, readers learned more about the character of Standard English (that it is primarily a matter of written conventions, used in school and business situations), the authors' views on nonstandardized varieties of English (that they are not wrong but may be inappropriate for certain situations), and the reasons why it is important for students to learn Standard English (to become strong, flexible communicators). As the text stated, "Nobody needs to use standard English all the time, but everybody should be able to use it when it is the right variety to use" (Odell et al., 2007, p. 941).

Some grammar books and style manuals do an excellent job of pointing out that many of the "rules" of Standard English are debatable or fluid. The well known grammar and style mavens, William Strunk Jr. and E.B. White, expressed the following flexible attitude toward prepositions in the 2000 edition of *The Elements of Style*: "Years ago, students were warned not to end a sentence with a preposition; time, of course, has softened that rigid decree. Not only is the preposition acceptable at the end, sometimes it is more effective in that spot than anywhere else" (pp. 77–78). On split infinitives they made a similar statement, saying, "The split infinitive is another trick of rhetoric in which the ear must be quicker than the handbook. Some infinitives seem to improve on being split" (p. 78).

Similarly, on the companion Web site for *A Pocket Style Manual* (Hacker, 2008), a section titled Language Debates offers commentary on rules such as the use of *who* versus *whom* (Hacker, n.d.). Hacker explains that while many "diehard purists" teach rules for when to use *who* and *whom*, it is also the case that for many speakers and listeners, *whom* often sounds pretentiously correct." Ideas and rules about the use of English change over time, based on many factors including the speaker, the audience, the content of the message, and the specific context in which the message is delivered.

Although Strunk and White (2000) and Hacker (2008) addressed changing language styles and conventions in general, they did not delve into issues surrounding language variation. It is necessary to teach students the conventions of standardized English, but it is also critical to teach students that nonstandardized varieties of English play important roles in society. Discussions of how politics, history, and culture have played a role in setting language standards and affecting attitudes about language help students understand the social context of their English language instruction. We maintain that students benefit from learning about language variation and understanding that all varieties, not just the standardized variety, are valuable in different ways. This goal parallels the tenets of multicultural education, which maintain that we must learn about ourselves as well as others.

Our Multicultural Approach

Grammar and language arts textbooks and style guides take a variety of approaches, some much more linguistically informed than others, in teaching standardized English to students at all grade levels. As we noted above, many textbooks exhibit what might be considered a traditional attitude about standardized English, contending that standardized English is the one correct and true form of English for students to learn and use. Vague approaches to describing language variation often result in inconsistent, misleading terminology and *you know it when you see it* definitions that make teaching and learning English language standards unnecessarily difficult and confusing for both educators and students.

In addition, textbooks with a traditional approach to language and grammar often adhere to the position that it is never appropriate to use nonstandardized English forms in formal settings, such as in courtrooms or on the political stage, but this claim is not true. Some traditional discussions further imply that if people are educated and native speakers of English, they could not possibly also speak a nonstandardized variety of English, which is a harmful idea to impart to students. In other textbooks, information about language variation may be simplified, scant, or omitted altogether.

Throughout this book, we explain ways to adopt linguistically informed ways of teaching standardized English. We advocate an understanding of when and how standardized English is best used as well as knowledge of how the structure and use of standardized English compare to the structure and use of nonstandardized varieties of English that students may use at home. The National Council of Teachers of English and the International Reading Association (1996) have endorsed this approach. These organizations have advocated that students learn to communicate effectively in what they call the "language of wider communication," or standardized English. To add standardized English to their linguistic repertoire, students should be encouraged to "engage in discussions of when and where this language of wider communication can and should be used." Through this process, students "further their knowledge of audience, purpose, and context, and in so doing discover something of the social significance of different language practices" (p. 34).

The National Council of Teachers of English and the International Reading Association (1996) also laid out broad standards for language arts education. Standard Nine held that students must "develop an understanding of and respect for diversity in language use, patterns, and dialects across cultures, ethnic groups, geographic regions, and social roles" (p. 41). The organizations explained:

> Language is a powerful medium through which we develop social and cultural understanding, and the need to foster this understanding is growing increasingly urgent as our culture becomes more diverse. . . . Schools are responsible for creating a climate of respect for the variety of languages that students speak and the variety of cultures from which they come. (pp. 41–42)

Our multicultural approach to teaching the conventions of standardized English, and to language more generally, includes four key elements. First, it is critical to specifically discuss with students the concept of *standardized English*. Such discussions should include the fact that standardized English is considered to be the variety of privilege and prestige and that standardized English has acquired its prestigious status due to the influence of powerful decision makers, including dictionary writers, educators, and politicians.

Second, we advocate the importance of explicitly teaching students the specific rules, norms, conventions, patterns, and features that constitute standardized English and also helping students learn the differences between standardized English and the language varieties that they bring with them from home. In this process, educators guide students in comparing and contrasting features and patterns from both varieties, using strategies such as those we suggest throughout this book.

Third, we find it necessary for educators to understand students' linguistic backgrounds and patterns in their communication styles. This pedagogical process includes recognizing where potential student errors are actually examples of language variation rather than evidence of language problems or persistent careless mistakes. When educators categorize language variations as errors in students' writing, oral reading, or speech, particularly without careful explanation as to why the student made a given mistake, students may become alienated from reading and writing processes. In fact, correcting students without explaining why they have made errors in standardized English has been found to result in *more* errors being made, not fewer (Piestrup, 1973). Instead, educators can use specific linguistic strategies, such as those we provide in this book, to guide students to recognize the differences in their speech, oral reading, and writing patterns as compared with those of standardized English.

Fourth, we believe educators who foster positive attitudes toward language and language variation help all students and educators develop an appreciation for the richness of language. Through such measures, educators and students of diverse language backgrounds will become more aware and respectful of language differences, both in their own communication patterns and in those of others.

SOME FEATURES OF SCHOOL ENGLISH

Proceeding from our multicultural approach, we advocate the explicit instruction of the important rules, norms, and conventions of standardized English in ways that are linguistically informed. As Schleppegrell (2001) explained: "Not all children come to school equally prepared to use language in the expected ways, nor do all share the same understanding that certain ways of using language are expected at school" (p. 434). Some students learn the standardized ways they are supposed to speak and write in school before they ever enter a classroom. Other students, even if they are from standardized English–speaking backgrounds, may not always know the linguistic conventions they need to use in school, and they have to learn them there. Some students may not learn these conventions at all, which may cause conflict in school settings and hinder these students' chances for academic success. With a greater understanding of what linguistic features students are expected to know and use at school, educators can better address how students learn standardized English and help them succeed throughout their academic careers.

In this section, we focus specifically on one kind of standardized English: *School English*, or the kind of standardized English that is specifically called for when students are at school. Just as we might refer to Business English as being a type of standardized English used in some segments of the business world, School English refers to the type of standardized English used in educational settings. School English is a standardized variety of English that must be learned, just as Business English is.

School English may look a bit different from school to school. The type of School English that is taught in elementary and middle school is simpler than what is taught in high school, college, and graduate school. In addition, School English might sound different when it is used in different places. For example, the School English that is spoken in a classroom in Charleston, South Carolina, will be a Southern-influenced standardized variety. As a result, the School English heard in Charleston will sound qualitatively different from the kind of English heard in classrooms in Albuquerque, New Mexico; Boston, Massachusetts; Detroit, Michigan; Seattle, Washington; and everywhere in between. Even if School English is spoken with an accent, it is still spoken in a standardized way that may differ from the local varieties of English spoken in the area.

As we use it in this book, *School English* is a situated term that captures the nuances surrounding how students and educators use standardized English in educational settings. Within the linguistic culture of every school setting and every content area, students are expected to learn and adhere to specific language-related academic norms. These norms, standards, and targets may differ across educational settings, and they may be influenced by the linguistic norms of given schools and communities. For schools to strip away all local accents and local linguistic features should be neither an expected outcome of the educational process nor a desired one.

Above all, instruction will benefit from an understanding of the features of School English as well as the features of the language varieties that students speak. For this reason, we now characterize and describe several important features of School English before discussing nonstandardized varieties of English in Chapters 3 and 4.

Don't Mumble

Students are often encouraged to be articulate and not to mumble, but they may not understand what such directives mean. While there is no specific linguistic definition for what it means to be articulate and to not mumble, the concept refers to clearly producing all of the sounds of a word and pronouncing them in phonetically standardized ways. Educators typically are supposed to adhere to these conventions as well.

There are many places in words where pronunciation differences might occur that might be perceived as mumbling. Final consonant blends are often not produced in English words. Most speakers of standardized English reduce some of the consonant sounds in clusters like *sk, nd, ts, kt, sts,* and *sks* when they occur at the ends of words, such that "Clean up under your *desks*" may sound similar to "Clean up under your *dess*"; "Put my Halloween *mask* down" may sound similar to "Put my Halloween *mass* down"; and "Please write in a less *abstract* way" may sound similar to "Please write in a less *abstrack* way." This phenomenon, known as consonant cluster reduction, occurs in all varieties of English, some more than others (Guy, 1980). For almost everyone, consonant cluster reduction occurs more often in casual and rapid speech than in slow and deliberate speech.

Another example of a similar phenomenon concerns the pronunciation of final *-g* sounds in words ending in *-ing* (Fischer, 1958). Throughout the United States, speakers commonly pronounce words that end in *-ing* as if they ended in *-in*. Words such as *running* may be alternately pronounced as "runnin'," *walking* as "walkin'," and *eating* as "eatin'." In rapid or casual speech, almost everyone uses *-in* for *-ing* at some point. When asking students to "pronounce their final *g*'s," it is important to remember that students are not being lazy or careless when alternating *-in* for *-ing*. Rather, their pronunciations are a regular manifestation of a linguistic alternation of two different sounds.

Another feature that contributes to perceptions of articulateness is the alternation of *a* and *an*. The conventions of standardized English state that the article *a* should be pronounced as *an* when the following word starts with a vowel. For example, if students say, "One day I saw *a eagle,*" they may be critiqued for not speaking in a standardized way. In casual environments, however, many speakers of English do not strictly follow the standardized English rule. Educators may need to explicitly explain to students that the alternation of *a* and *an* is an important feature of School English, as well as a feature that relates to how other people perceive a speaker's eloquence outside of school settings.

Students may need to be told explicitly when certain features should be avoided. Students may need to be told that when they hear "Use careful words" or "Be careful with your pronunciation," the target may be the need to avoid reducing clusters of consonants at the ends of words, for example, or to avoid using *-in* for *-ing*. Educators can also review with students common oratorical conventions that students are expected to adhere to when speaking in front of a class, giving an academic presentation, saying their part in a school play, or speaking as part of the Debate Club. Students can be taught that it may be necessary to pronounce final consonant blends and *-ing* sounds to sound eloquent in these settings.

Some students, in reaction to messages about articulation, may begin to overcorrect and try to pronounce all the sounds in words. Some students, for example, may pronounce words like *butter* with the *t*'s fully aspirated, rather than pronouncing the word like "budder," as most speakers of standardized English do. Students may also hyperarticulate by pronouncing letters that are silent in standardized pronunciations. Words such as *folk, yolk, talk,* and *walk,* which generally have silent *l*'s in standardized English, may be pronounced with the *l*'s intact by speakers who are trying hard to not skip over any sounds. Hyperarticulation may sound odd to listeners, and students who hypercorrect may be teased for talking too properly or for using a style that seems out of place.

STRATEGIES FOR EDUCATORS

Goodman (2003) suggested that students list the characteristics of oral reading and public speaking that engage them most when they are listening. Students will offer qualities like having a strong voice, changing one's voice to represent different characters, and enunciating clearly. Students can develop a list of their own best practices for elocution and implement them, and educators can model these best practices. Working with students to understand what counts as speaking eloquently will eliminate any mystique surrounding this concept and provide ways for students to practice specific features and forms.

Students may also mumble because they are insecure or feel nervous about speaking up in educational settings, and all students may need more time to become confident about sharing their opinions and answers out loud. As Dickmann, Stanford-Blair, and Rosati-Bojar (2004) described, students in school settings may ask themselves, "Am I safe here, and will I be successful?" For nonstandardized English–speaking students, there is an added dimension when they are asked to engage with educators using School English. These students may need to interpret the School English they hear from their educators and peers, and they may need time to formulate what they intend to say into a School English format. In other words, some students may need to perform "translations" that may take more time than other students require. It is important to actively respect this extra challenge and allow time for these complex linguistic processes to occur. For nonstandardized English–speaking students to feel that they are safe and that they can be successful in school situations, they must feel that they will not be ridiculed as they strive to communicate in the School English that is required of them.

STRATEGIES FOR EDUCATORS

When a question is asked, all students need time to hear the question, interpret the query, recall relevant information, and sequence the response using appropriate vocabulary—all while considering whether or not to even raise their hand and answer. Additional challenges may face nonstandardized English–speaking students, who may need extra time to formulate their answers in School English. To help encourage all students to speak up, confidently answer questions, and participate in discussions, educators may need to add wait time to their questions.

Cazden (1990) suggested that educators implement a "take a minute and think" rule in the classroom to allow all students time to plan their answers and/or to allow educators to call on a wider variety of students. Lyman (1981) suggested that educators could provide students with time to "think, pair, share," a process in which students think about the question, reach a conclusion in their heads, share ideas with a partner, and then share responses with the group. Employing these and similar strategies may help all students, especially nonstandardized English–speaking students, participate in educational settings and listen and respond to all their peers. For more strategies on facilitating classroom discourse, also see Michaels, O'Connor, and Resnick (2008).

Don't Write Like You Talk

When students write like they talk, transferring forms from spoken to written English, challenges may arise regardless of what language background the students are from. The use of sentence fragments and the overuse of the passive voice may give students trouble at the sentence level. Nonstandardized subject–verb agreement, verb tenses, adjectives and adverbs, double or multiple negatives, pronouns, and many other grammatical issues challenge students in all grades of school and later in life. More subtle issues like misplaced modifiers, where to use apostrophes, and how to use quotation marks may, from time to time, confront even the most advanced writer.

Not writing the way one talks includes using academic vocabulary, but students may not understand how their everyday vocabulary is different from the vocabulary that is expected to be used in school settings. School English, both written and spoken, tends to use vocabulary items that are more literary than colloquial, such as *entrance* rather than *door*, *employ* rather than *use*, *beginning* rather than *start*, *collaborate* rather than *work together*, and *acquire* rather than *get*. Indeed, from elementary school spelling tests, to vocabulary questions on standardized tests, to Word-a-Day calendars for adults, cultural indicators suggest that to be educated in our society is to have a big vocabulary. Yet students may not have been taught explicitly about contrasts in vocabulary words, the notion of register, and the concept of diction, all of which are vocabulary and stylistic choices that writers and speakers make. It is therefore important to instruct students whenever possible as to differences between academic terms and colloquial terms for the same concepts.

Focusing students' attention on vocabulary can start on the most basic level, as even simple words, such as conjunctions, can cause students trouble in their learning of School English. Scarborough and colleagues (2003) found that when some kindergartners begin school, they are much more familiar than others with certain conjunctions, prepositions, pronouns, adverbs, and adjectives that are used to refer to relationships between objects and events. These types of words, called relational words, are typically used in classroom instruction and assessment. A chart of common relational words is provided in Figure 2.1.

Relational words may be difficult for students because many relational terms can express the same idea, but all terms may not be part of every student's linguistic background. The words that are given first in the following list are characteristic of School English, while the words in parentheses are characteristic of everyday language: *beginning* (*first, start*); *along the lines of* (*like*); *as a matter of fact* (*in fact, in reality, actually*); *primary* (*first*); *secondary* (*second*); *behind* (*in back of*); *probably* (*maybe*); *exactly as* (*just like*); *ending* (*last*); and *concluding* (*last*). Students are likely to be much more familiar with everyday ways of saying what the School English terms also express.

Relational words are critically important to learning School English because these words are used in building reading fluency and reading comprehension skills, as well as in test instructions and assignments across all subject areas. In elementary school classrooms—during lessons, storybook read-alouds, or other activities—educators may use sentences

Figure 2.1. Common relational words.

Space	*Time*	*Order*	*Quantity*	*Logic*
top	until	first	all (of)	same
bottom	when	last	every	alike
up	whenever	second	each (of)	similar
down	soon	third (etc.)	most (of)	different
above	later	beginning	many (of)	opposite
below	early	end(ing)	much (of)	exactly
over	always	middle	some (of)	almost
under	forever	next	several (of)	nearly
underneath	ever	next to last	(a) few (of)	quite
beneath	never	from . . . to	a little	somewhat
upside-down	often	before	any	very
(in) front (of)	usually	after	more	probably
(in) back (of)	still		less	if ... then
left (of)			none (of)	because
right (of)			no	so
			total	whether
				or
				unless
				therefore

Source: Scarborough et al., 2003.

such as "What did the lion do at the *beginning* of the story," "Tell me *some* things that Sasha found *behind* the door," and "Put a mark next to *each* object that has the 'mmm' sound." Students who do not understand these relational terms may be hindered in learning to read or comprehend reading passages because they do not understand what the instructor is telling them or asking them to do.

When Scarborough and colleagues (2003) gave groups of kindergartners and first-graders of low socioeconomic status a 32-item Comprehension of Relational Terms (CORT) test, they investigated how young students interpret instructions containing relational terms. In one exercise, the evaluator gave students instructions that contained relational terms, such as, "Point to the picture that shows the cat that is *on top of* the chair. Now point to the cat that is *in front of* the chair." Most of the terms referring to spatial relationships were well understood, but many other relational terms were not. Notably, the terms *beginning, middle, end, exactly the same, a few of,* and *most of* were not comprehended by many kindergartners. By first grade, most students vastly improved their understanding of relational terms, but for other students, many relational terms remained incomprehensible, even after a year of schooling.

When Scarborough and colleagues (2003) trained teachers to use the CORT to evaluate their own students' use of relational items, many teachers were astonished by the data. One teacher, after administering the CORT to her class, phoned Anne in distress and said, "I can't believe it. I've been teaching reading for 15 years. I've been saying things like, 'What happened at the beginning of the story?' and 'Pay attention to the beginning of the word,' and today I discovered that half my class has no clue what *beginning* means! If only I had known. It's so easy to *fix*!"

Relational terms are also used in many standardized assessments of early literacy skills, as in the following sentences from various published tests: "What's the *beginning* sound in the word 'go'?" "Can you find *any* words you can read?" "Say it *exactly* as you hear it." "Say the word *one sound at a time, without my prompting you.*" Students who are familiar with relational terms and who are well versed in School English have a distinct advantage on these assessments, just as they may have a distinct advantage in their classrooms when they learn to read and when they follow instructions from their educators.

When teaching vocabulary, it is important to make no assumptions as to what vocabulary items students already know. The need to explain academic vocabulary items persists at all educational levels. The idea that there are academic ways of expressing familiar meanings and conventions for when to write in an academic tone must be explained to students throughout their academic careers.

STRATEGIES FOR EDUCATORS

In addition to school-specific vocabulary, academic jargon is increasingly found across the educational spectrum. Students and educators alike must learn a range of education-related jargon, from such words and phrases as *briefly constructed responses* and *power writing* to *data-driven* and *21st-century learning*. These words often rapidly come into vogue, and for those who have not had these terms explained to them, their meanings and connotations may be hard to discern. Similarly, jargon developed within the spheres of computer science, information technology, medicine, law, and other fields is generally unfamiliar to outsiders and must be learned in a direct manner.

It is best for educators to explicitly discuss with students the types of jargon that they are expected to learn and use in school, and educators may model for students how to phrase or rephrase their statements using academic jargon. Such scaffolding techniques support students' learning (Mehan, 1979). For all students, exposure to academic jargon and to the specific linguistic conventions used in educational settings is essential for student success.

Sometimes, students who try to use complex words and phrases to enhance their writing end up hypercorrecting. Hypercorrection is a common response among students who are so aware of the pitfalls of writing below grade level, and so leery of writing the same way they talk, that they go overboard (Odlin, 1989). Students who hypercorrect may use words such as *conversate* and *orientate*, which are word formations that have been created by analogy, in a process that linguists call "back formation." Just as the verb *communicate* is a form of the noun *communication*, for example, speakers of English have derived the verb *conversate* from the noun *conversation* and, similarly, *orientate* from *orientation*. Sometimes new words that are formed through back formation have been adopted as part of standardized English vocabulary; for example, the verb *enthuse* was derived from the noun *enthusiasm*. In other cases, public opinion may deem words like *conversate* and *orientate* to be unnecessary, because other standardized English words already exist that mean the same thing (e.g., *converse, orient*). All languages have the flexibility in their vocabulary systems to support multiple words that mean the same thing. Nevertheless, there are often strong social conventions and opinions surrounding whether new words are considered to be socially acceptable. Students who are only aware of a nonstandardized, innovative variant (e.g., *conversate*) can be explicitly taught that a standardized variant of the same word exists (e.g., *converse*) and that it may be considered more socially acceptable in standardized contexts.

Students may also use academic words that over time have become overused, including *ameliorate, peruse*, and *per se*. They may use extended noun phrases, such as "The fact of the matter is that" or "The thing is, is that." They may mix up word forms, such as using a noun when an adjective is needed: "Most dieters are not *persistence* enough" instead of "Most dieters are not *persistent* enough." Some students may also use clichés and overused expressions in an attempt to sound formal. Just as some students need to be taught that there are more formal ways of saying the same thing, other students may be helped to understand that complex, multisyllabic words are not the only way to signal that a piece of writing is academic in nature.

STRATEGIES FOR EDUCATORS

Smith and Wilhelm (2007) suggested that when students need help revising their writing, educators can focus on addressing one or two language patterns at a time, making sure students understand why they tend to use these specific patterns, before moving on to new challenges. They stated, "Instead of worrying about every error in every paper, we think it makes far more sense to focus our own and our students' attention on one issue at a time. It means modeling, mentoring, and monitoring student practice until they truly understand how a language convention works and can really use it correctly" (p. 61).

The "paramedic method" (Brizee, 2007) is also an excellent way to help students learn to edit their own writing for conciseness. Style manuals and writer reference tools, such as Strunk and White's *Elements of Style* (2000) and the MLA and Chicago style guides, may help explain to students the conventions for producing standardized writing.

It is also important to provide students models of writing samples for graded writing assignments. Educators may provide examples of A papers, B papers, and so on, and discuss with students how factors such as grammatical features, vocabulary choices, sentence structure, and essay length contribute to each grade. Peer revising can also build students' language awareness. Goodman (2003) and Andrews (2006) suggested encouraging students to document their own spelling and grammar patterns in journals. Keeping journals can help students monitor conventions of standardized English that are challenging to them.

One-on-one educator–student conferences are essential, and it is necessary to be familiar with the different nonstandardized English features that are likely to appear in students' writing. In a language variation workshop we held with educators, many participants shared that they already hold one-on-one conferences with their students, even in kindergarten.

In addition to having a large academic vocabulary, the conventions for conversing and writing in School English include specific notions of clarity and style. "Writing like you talk" may cause nonstandardized English–speaking students in particular to be overpenalized in assessments of their writing, and these students may be told as early as pre-kindergarten that their writing does not make sense. When students use nonstandardized English features in their writing, their writing may erroneously be perceived as nonlinear, nonconceptual, and illogical. Such students may also receive such comments on their compositions as "Your writing is all over the place," "This doesn't make sense," or "You need to write this in *standard* English" with very little explanation as to why, making for a frustrating academic experience. Many common grammatical errors that are often marked in students' work are, in fact, regular and patterned nonstandardized English features, many of which we discuss in later chapters in this book. Language variations can be pointed out to students and compared and contrasted with the features that are used in School English, and educators can model how they expect students to communicate in different situations. Above all, specificity matters when teaching students about expectations for writing and speaking in School English.

Don't Take That Tone with Me

Tone of voice can convey a range of emotions, including enthusiasm, anger, anxiety, and boredom. Even though tone matters a great deal, in School English as well as in work and in everyday life, explicitly teaching about tone is often overlooked in education. Intonation patterns in standardized English are closely tied to politeness and emotion, but students who are less familiar with standardized patterns of intonation may inadvertently express boredom, disinterest, or displeasure.

Students may also be chastised for the use of nonstandardized intonation patterns. For example, students may frequently produce statements with the final high-rising intonation pattern that, in standardized English, is used for questions. Many adults criticize or disparage this linguistic feature when students use it in situations in which they are not intending to ask a question (Eckert & McConnell-Ginet, 2003). A student who is perceived to be saying "My name is Jenny? And I'm in sixth grade?" rather than "My name is Jenny, and I'm in sixth grade" may be thought of by adults as uncertain, approval-seeking, silly, nervous, airheaded, or unintelligent, rather than simply speaking with an intonation pattern that has become very widespread among her peer group.

The volume and pitch of students' voices, as well as their rate of speech, also play a crucial role in how students are expected to express themselves in School English. Students are often urged to make a distinction between their inside and outside voices, and educators may actively discourage such behaviors as yelling, whining, and speaking in a high pitch. Some students may also be chided for speaking too slowly or too quickly, too loudly or too softly. Typically, the conventions of School English suggest that speech should be delivered at a moderate volume. Students who do not adhere to these expectations may be told to "Please speak up," "Talk louder," "Use your inside voice," and "Speak clearly," but it is imperative to discuss with students exactly what these requests mean and why they are being made.

The typical conventions of School English also dictate that students should speak and read at a constant pace, and students are encouraged to vary their intonation patterns. Fluency is often measured in oral reading by listening to the rhythm and melody of the student's reading voice. Speech rate may be a particularly challenging issue for students who speak Southern English, however, as Southern speakers have been found to speak at a slightly slower rate than students from other regions. Educators (and students themselves) may hold negative stereotypes that Southerners who are slower talkers are also slower, less intelligent thinkers; it is critical to dispel this harmful misconception.

The words that students use can also affect how educators perceive students' tone. When students answer "yeah" instead of "yes," or "uh-uh" instead of "no," they may be perceived as being rude or inappropriate. In reality, students may simply be answering in a more colloquial style, and they may never have been taught that School English generally requires students to answer with "yes" rather than "yeah" (or, in the South, with "Yes, ma'am" and "Yes, sir") and "no" (or "No, ma'am" and "No, sir") rather than "uh-uh." Students also may not know that educators expect them to say "Excuse me?" rather than "What?" or "Huh?" when they are asked a question but need something repeated, and they may not know that certain linguistic features, such as the fillers *like* and *um*, are not received favorably by educators at school (despite the fact that, at home or outside of school settings, educators themselves may frequently use these same language variants).

STRATEGIES FOR EDUCATORS

Educators may help students acquire School English–specific norms for classroom discourse by developing a poster to put up on the wall or a handout to give to students that models how students are expected to ask and answer questions at school (e.g., "excuse me" for "huh" or "what," "no" rather than "uh-uh," and so on). Educators can also explicitly discuss with students the kind of tone, speech rate, and volume they expect them to use in the classroom—for example, when asking questions, reading out loud, and telling stories. Educators and students can discuss the fact that School English conventions may vary from the ways that students and educators communicate outside the classroom. It is crucial to show respect for students' home language varieties while helping students develop familiarity with School English.

Classroom Language

The term *register* refers to how the use of language varies according to a particular social situation or social context. For many students, learning the conventions of School English has a great deal to do with proper register selection; indeed, Martin (1983) calls the development of register the most important aspect of language development that occurs after age 5. For example, the language of a science report is different from that of an essay about a novel and that of a math problem set. Students are expected to learn each of these registers and the fact that different subjects require different terminology.

STRATEGIES FOR EDUCATORS

Goodman (2003) suggested that educators ask students to describe, record, analyze, and interpret how their language is the same or different when they do a range of activities, including giving a class presentation or report, arguing, talking on the phone, greeting friends, greeting family members, and greeting educators. Andrews (2006) also described an "On the Job Talking" exercise in which students discuss registers used in job situations. These exercises can enhance students' awareness of register.

School English requires that students address educators in certain school-specific ways. Forms like *Principal Carter, Miss Pamela, Mrs. Daniels,* and *Dr. B* are a few examples of how to address educators in a school register. Such forms are called *honorifics,* which are words or phrases that are used to address or refer to other people and that generally convey a sense of esteem or respect. Common honorifics in English are *Ms., Mrs., Mr., Dr., ma'am, sir,* and *Professor*. Some educators and students may have differing opinions and conventions as to which honorifics should be used and when. Educators can specifically discuss with students their opinions surrounding the use of honorifics, including whether or not students should call educators by their first names. These conventions can be contrasted with how students typically address each other in the classroom and how they address their family members and friends, thereby building students' awareness of honorifics as an element of School English.

Students must also understand educators' ways of conversing in School English if they are to succeed. To students, educators may speak slowly and loudly, or sometimes they may whisper to get students' attention. They may also use dynamic patterns of intonation and emphasis, as in the sentence, "I *like* how Jeremy is speaking *quietly* and doing a *great job* on his *homework*!" These stress and pitch patterns differ greatly from how most educators speak when they are outside school settings. It is important not to assume that students understand what educators' use of emphasis and pitch means, as not every student will understand without instruction.

Cazden (2001) examined the ways educators and students talk to each other in the classroom and found that many educators use classroom-specific phrases. Phrases such as "Please summarize," "Give me an educated guess," "Can anybody tell us the answer?" and "Any questions so far?" are aimed at encouraging students to answer questions. To manage student behavior, educators may use classroom-specific phrases such as "Boys and girls," "Are we using our inside voices?," "Settle down," "1, 2, 3, eyes on me," "I'll wait," and "Take your seats." Some of these School English phrases and idioms might be difficult for students to understand if they are not familiar with the conventions of School English, and thus students may need these phrases to be carefully explained.

In addition to hearing these specific types of School English phrases, students are often used to being asked "known-answer" questions, which require them to state answers that are known to the question asker as well as to students. For example, a lesson on dictionaries may begin with the question, "Class, what kind of book is this?" As many educators are aware, students may not always respond when they are asked these types of questions. Students' lack of response, however, is not necessarily a result of their not knowing the answer. In some cases, known-answer questions may violate students' views of the purpose of using language and asking questions. If students know that an educator knows the answer to the question that was asked, they may not see the point of stating the obvious. If students understand the point of a question right away, they also may not feel the need to answer by pointing out the obvious and so may lose interest in the lesson. Such miscommunication can create serious challenges for students. In many educational situations, a lack of response may give the false impression that students do not understand simple questions, which may lead to frustrations for educators as well as students.

There are many cultural and social reasons why students may want to sound distinctly different from educators. The general lack of male educators may pose an impossible linguistic situation for male students who do not want to sound like their female educators yet do not have many male educator role models. Some boys may resist the word choices, pronunciations, speech rate, volume, pitch, and tempo that are being advocated by their female educators in an effort to get them to adapt to School English norms.

When students are not White and middle class and their educators are, students may face similar language-related issues. Students may get reprimanded for misbehaving, for disrespecting their classmates, or for taking an inappropriate tone with an educator. Students may also receive lower marks in participation because they do not respond to educators' questions or because they read or participate in a monotonous voice. Solutions for these problems include not only explicitly teaching conventions for School English features, such as tone, but also increased understanding, awareness, and sensitivity on the part of educators.

Learning to become versatile in School English is necessary for academic success. Students need guidance to attain specific knowledge about the features and intricacies that make up School English, and it is best to communicate this information from a positive point of view. All students with this knowledge and understanding will be better equipped to become more versatile in School English, expand their standardized English repertoire, and respect all language variation and diversity in educational settings and beyond.

AN EDUCATOR'S PERSPECTIVE

"In the past, I never realized that School English needs to be taught explicitly. Now, I understand that language protocol is not innate. For some children, School English, including the use of honorifics and appropriate verbal responses, needs to be part of the curriculum."

THE PRIVILEGE OF STANDARDIZED ENGLISH

We have discussed how students who come to school speaking nonstandardized forms of English and who do not already know the norms, conventions, and rules of School English are at a *disadvantage*. In contrast, students who come to school speaking and writing in standardized ways and knowing the norms, conventions, and rules of School English have several *advantages* and *privileges*. We have created a short list of what we call "standardized English privileges," provided in Figure 2.2. We suggest that speakers of standardized English enjoy many linguistic privileges included in "invisible dictionaries" that they carry. Our concept is based on McIntosh (1988), and we have adapted some of the privileges we list from a discussion provided in Chen-Hayes, Chen, and Athar (1999).

Through listing these privileges, we do not blame speakers of standardized English for having socially conferred advantages. Rather, as Chen-Hayes and colleagues (1999) stated, it is important that educators, students, administrators, parents, staff, and others be aware of issues of privilege so that everyone can advocate for linguistic diversity and linguistic tolerance. The message in all educational settings should be, "Here we listen to what everyone has to say, no matter how they say it." Throughout this book, we provide evidence that English language variation occurs normally and naturally and that nonstandardized varieties of English deserve not stigmatization, but rather understanding and respect.

Figure 2.2. Seven privileges of standardized English.

1. Standardized English–speaking students can usually be assured that the newspapers, magazines, books, and other media they encounter at school will be in the type of English they are already familiar with.
2. Standardized English–speaking students can usually be assured that they will not be mocked or teased for how they pronounce their words.
3. Standardized English–speaking students can usually be assured that they will not be thought of as being less intelligent because of how they talk.
4. Standardized English–speaking students can usually be assured that standardized test instructions and materials will be written in the English they are already familiar with.
5. Standardized English–speaking students can usually be assured that most of their educators will communicate with them in the type of English the students are already familiar with.
6. Standardized English–speaking students can generally be assured that the way they talk will not be the subject of jokes or belittling in mainstream TV shows or movies.
7. Standardized English–speaking students can generally be assured that their pronunciation, intonation, and sentence structure will not interfere with their ability to be assessed accurately, to interact with authority figures, or, later in life, to obtain housing and be hired for a job.

3

Southern English: A Regional and Cultural Variety

SOUTHERN ENGLISH is spoken by a wide range of people from the South, from everyday citizens to the political and cultural elite. Southern elements are heard in the speech of Presidents Jimmy Carter, Bill Clinton, and George W. Bush and in the sermons of famous ministers, including Billy Graham, Jesse Jackson, and Martin Luther King Jr. Southern English is also notable in the speech of many popular media figures, including Dixie Carter, Matthew McConaughey, Billy Bob Thornton, Oprah Winfrey, and Reese Witherspoon. Southern culture, linguistic and otherwise, is also prevalent in the lyrics of entertainers, from country music stars such as Garth Brooks, the Dixie Chicks, Dolly Parton, and Elvis Presley; to gospel music singers such as Aretha Franklin and Mahalia Jackson; to hip-hop artists such as Ludacris and the duo OutKast.

Speakers of Southern English make up the largest accent group in the United States (MacNeil & Cran, 2005). As Jonsson (2007) reported, the huge population migration to the South that began in the 1940s and the increasing national appeal of country music, in which Southern accents play a central role, are two primary factors that have brought attention to and popularized Southern English. Yet despite the strong influence of Southern history, language, and lifestyle on the American cultural scene, Southern English is one of the most denigrated and stigmatized language varieties in the United States. With a history marked by slavery, an agrarian economy, the Civil War, segregation, and political and religious conservatism, the South has often been called an old-fashioned, traditional region that is short on economic and cultural progress. Southern people have often been regarded as racist, lazy, uneducated, and slow, and, in the same way, the language that marks the people of this region is thought by many people to be proof of Southerners' backward nature.

We maintain that understanding Southern culture and language is critical to understanding and serving Southern students. In this chapter, we explore the history of Southern English and delve into the sensitive topic of attitudes and stereotypes surrounding this regional and cultural variety of English, especially with regard to how these views impact Southern students. Given the large and growing population of Southern students, it is necessary to understand Southern culture and the South's linguistic heritage. With this knowledge and awareness, educators can best serve students who come to school speaking Southern English. With the understanding that Southern English variations are not random, incorrect sounds or grammatical errors, greater respect for Southerners' linguistic and cultural heritage is communicated. Linguistically informed educators are also better equipped to instruct students about the similarities of and differences between Southern English and standardized English, thereby empowering students to value their home language patterns and learn the linguistic norms and conventions that enable them to master standardized English.

DEFINING THE SOUTH

The South is the nation's most populous region, home to 36% of all Americans, or approximately 110 million residents (U.S. Census Bureau, 2006). According to the U.S. Census, the South includes Florida, Georgia, North Carolina, South Carolina, Virginia, West Virginia, Maryland, Washington, D.C., and Delaware (the South Atlantic states); Alabama, Kentucky, Mississippi, and Tennessee (the East South Central states); and Arkansas, Louisiana, Oklahoma, and Texas (the West South Central states).

Popular definitions of the South may differ from the U.S. Census Bureau's definition. For some, the South is found anywhere south of the Mason-Dixon Line and east of the Mississippi. For others, the South includes all of the states that were designated slave states or border states during the Civil War. A cultural approach may also be used to define the South. Some popular definitions exclude northern Virginia on the grounds that it has become an annex of Washington, D.C. Other definitions exclude parts of Florida and Texas on the grounds that southern Florida is heavily populated by Northern retirees and all but the eastern part of Texas has a Southwestern-influenced culture. In contrast, very broad definitions of the South include southern parts of Illinois, Indiana, and Ohio, since the language and culture of these states may ring Southern as well.

The South is now increasing in population size, "attracting a diverse populace" while "increasingly holding on to its native flock" (Hunt, Hunt, & Falk, 2008, pp. 110, 114). More Americans, especially African Americans, are moving to the South from other parts of the country, and more Americans, especially African Americans, who had grown up in the South and moved away to pursue educational or occupational opportunities are deciding to move back to their Southern birth-states. Hunt and colleagues (2008) therefore predicted that the South will continue to be the most populated region of the United States for years to come.

LANGUAGE VARIATION IN THE SOUTH

As a heterogeneous region with a rich social, political, and cultural history, the South is home to many languages and language varieties that have influenced the development of Southern English. From the 16th century until the mid-18th century, the South was "a place where more different languages were spoken than anywhere else except California" (Rudes, 2004, p. 37). The linguistic diversity of the South persists and has shaped the many languages and language varieties spoken there.

Native American Influences

In the South, Native American history and culture dates back well over 10,000 years and continues to influence Southern language and culture today. Native American place names, such as Cataloochee, Chattanooga, Hiwassee, Oconoluftee, Okeechobee, Nantahala, Pensacola, and Tallahassee, are found throughout the South. Many words now common in English, including *chipmunk, hickory, hominy, moccasin, opossum,* and *pecan,* also reveal the linguistic legacy of Native Americans.

As a result of atrocities perpetrated against Native Americans throughout much of the history of the United States, the number of speakers of Native American languages drastically fell, and many of these languages became extinct. In 1990, the Native American Languages Act was passed to protect and promote Native Americans' right to speak their own languages. Although many Native American languages have been lost, the Cherokee language is still spoken throughout the territory that the Cherokee Nation calls the "Quallah Boundary," located in western North Carolina (Bender, 2002). Several schools have implemented Cherokee Language Immersion Programs to promote the use of the language by younger generations.

Cajun and Creole Influences

French and Spanish were brought to the South by 16th- and 17th-century explorers. In much of the Southeast, especially Florida and Louisiana, Spanish influenced the formation of different cultures and language varieties. The "Castilians," who have lived on an island in a bayou south of New Orleans, Louisiana, since the 1700s, speak one variety of Spanish; in Louisiana's Ascension Parish, some people speak Brule, a Spanish variety strongly influenced by Cajun French (Reed & Reed, 1996, pp. 28–29).

Cajun and Creole cultures in Louisiana developed out of African, Caribbean, French, and Spanish cultures. Many Cajun people speak a variety of French known as Cajun French, and many of them also speak a variety of English, known as Cajun English. The term *Creole* refers more specifically to "those of African or mixed-race ancestry . . . whose black or mulatto ancestors came to Louisiana in the late eighteenth century either as slaves of French planters or as *gens libre de couleur* fleeing the Haitian revolution" (Reed & Reed, 1996, p. 27). Creole populations throughout Louisiana also speak French and English.

African Influences

As North America was colonized, enslaved Africans were brought to the United States, especially to the region of the United States that is now considered to be the Deep South: South Carolina, Georgia, Alabama, Mississippi, and Louisiana. The influence of the languages that enslaved Africans spoke in their native countries has had a lasting effect on language variation throughout the South.

One particular influence can be seen in the language called *Gullah* (or *Geechee*), an African- and English-influenced language and culture that developed in the Sea Islands along the coast of South Carolina, Georgia, and northeast Florida. The isolation of these islands to which enslaved Africans were imported helped preserve the influence of African languages on Gullah. Comparative techniques reveal that Gullah is related to Jamaican Creole, Bahamian English, and the Krio language of Sierra Leone. The film *The Language You Cry In* (Toepke & Serrano, 1998) traced the history of a five-line Gullah song to its origins as a burial song in the Mende language of Sierra Leone.

Appalachia

According to the Appalachian Regional Commission (ARC homepage, n.d.), Appalachia has approximately 24 million residents. The 205,000-square-mile region includes West Virginia and parts of Alabama, Mississippi, Georgia, North Carolina, South Carolina, Virginia, Kentucky, Maryland, New York, Ohio, Pennsylvania, Tennessee, and Virginia.

Appalachian English is often noticed for its distinctive pronunciations. In Appalachia, words such as *pass* may be pronounced as "pace," and *grass* may be pronounced as "grace." The word *tire* may be pronounced as "tar," and *fire* may be pronounced as "far." Uniquely Appalachian words have also been coined. The term *jasper* refers to an outsider; *tee-totally* means "completely"; *sigogglin'* means "tilted, leaning, or crooked"; *Eh law!* is an expression meaning "Oh well!"; and a *young'un* refers to a child. The word *you'n* may also be used instead of *y'all*, and travelers to Appalachia may hear the question, "Where you'ns from?"

Because of the region's historical isolation from other parts of the United States, some people have suggested that Appalachian language patterns are similar to Elizabethan English or Old English. Montgomery (1999) explained, "The idea that in isolated places somewhere in the country people still use 'Elizabethan' or 'Shakespearean' speech is widely held, and it is probably one of the hardier cultural beliefs or myths in the collective American psyche" (p. 66). While Appalachian folks use some archaic English words (such as *nigh* for *near*), Appalachian English is not the same thing as Elizabethan or Shakespearean English. Appalachian English has had multiple linguistic influences, most notably the speech of migrants from Ulster, the northern province of Ireland (Montgomery, 1999). Appalachian English has also changed over time, inventing new words and colloquialisms specific to the region and culture.

A Diversifying South

Young, educated people from diverse racial and ethnic backgrounds are migrating to the South in increasing numbers, taking advantage of the greater economic opportunity and social equality that now exists there (Hunt et al., 2008). In addition to Washington, D.C., and Atlanta, Georgia, African Americans constitute the majority of the population and political force in Baltimore, Maryland; Richmond, Virginia; Birmingham, Alabama; Jackson, Mississippi; and New Orleans, Louisiana (Wickham, 2005).

The South has also seen a dramatic rise in immigration from outside the United States. According to the Pew Research Center (Kochhar, Suro, & Tafoya, 2005), the Hispanic population of North Carolina grew at a rate of nearly 400% between 1990 and 2000, the largest population growth in the United States during that period. Southern English and culture will blend and change as Latinos and Latinas continue to settle in the South and make the region their home.

Greater migration to the South may affect the character of local language varieties. Nevertheless, non-Southerners who move to the area may find that their children grow up sounding like Southerners. As Jonsson (2007) reported, identity features are "crucial in determining whether someone retains or loses an accent. That's why in rural areas of the South, Southern features are still pretty strong" (para. 22).

ATTITUDES TOWARD SOUTHERN ENGLISH

Although no one language variety is inherently better than any other, many people have strong beliefs about Southern English. Preston (1998) extensively researched people's ideas about language in the United States. When respondents were asked to rate the degree of "correctness" of English spoken in regions around the country, they repeatedly gave the South the lowest ratings—even when the respondents were Southerners themselves.

Reed (1992) also pointed out that a speaker's Southern accent may cause others to form negative stereotypes about that speaker's intelligence. Reed described experimental studies that found that the average non-Southern college sophomore assumes a Southern English speaker is less bright than a non-Southern English speaker, even when the two speakers are saying exactly the same thing. "Since college sophomores occasionally grow up to be employers," Reed noted, "it may make sense to take [these beliefs] into account" (p. 55). Reed further pointed out that, in the past, some members of Congress had even "specified 'no Southern accent' as a criterion for hiring folks to work in their offices" (p. 55).

Even in the country music world, having a Southern accent that is thought to be too strong may be stigmatized. Serrie (2002) reported that James Carney, a morning DJ for an Atlanta, Georgia, country music radio station, was fired because of his Southern accent. During the 11 years he worked there, Carney received numerous company memos asking him to take diction lessons and grammar lessons. He refused, and eventually he was fired. In fact, researchers have documented the link between lost income and speaking with a Southern accent. Grogger (2008) found that speakers who sound Southern earn salaries that are lower than workers with comparable skills who do not sound Southern, even if these speakers live in the South.

Speaking Southern English is not necessarily always a hindrance, however, as some jobs rely in part on sounding identifiably regional. Young (2008) profiled Joe Rice, a South Carolina lawyer, whose accent is credited with giving him an edge in the courtroom. Political leaders—including

Presidents Jimmy Carter, Bill Clinton, and George W. Bush; Senators Elizabeth Dole and Kay Bailey Hutchison; and Governor Ann Richards—have also used Southern English on a national stage to great appeal.

Lippi-Green (1997) and Preston (1998) found that although people tend to associate Southern English with low intelligence, quaintness, and incompetence, they also tend to associate it with pleasantness and friendliness. Soukup (2000) gave Southern and Northern respondents a hypothetical job interview scenario and asked them to listen to the voices of Southerners and Northerners. When asked which people they would rather hire, the respondents thought that the Southern English speakers would be less competent than the applicants who spoke "neutral English," and that they would therefore be less likely to hire the Southerners. The respondents also thought, however, that the female Southern voice sounded most favorable in terms of "personal interest." In many ways, characterizing Southern English as an improper yet friendly way of talking has become one socially acceptable way to construct cultural differences between the South and the rest of the United States, particularly the more urban Northeast.

STRATEGIES FOR EDUCATORS

The media are a rich, though sometimes stereotypical, source of portrayals of Southerners and Appalachian folk. Goodman (2003) suggested that students examine media representations of Southern English as a starting point for discussing language variation. Younger students may explore how characters' use of language affects their understanding of and their feelings about the characters or whether there are differences in the ways that language is used for some characters compared with others.

Older students may compare and contrast representations of Southern and Appalachian speech with their firsthand knowledge about these varieties and/or representations of other language varieties in literature. They may also explore the pros and cons of using spelling to represent variation in Southern English, as, for example, in books by authors such as William Faulkner, Toni Morrison, Mildred Taylor, and Mark Twain. They may also read from collections of Appalachian writers, such as Dyer (1998).

Older students may also benefit from viewing films about language variation in the South. *Mountain Talk* (Hutcheson, 2004) and *Voices of North Carolina* (Hutcheson, 2005) focus on Southern and Appalachian English, while *American Tongues*

(Alvarez & Kolker, 1988) and *Do You Speak American?* (MacNeil & Cran, 2005) discuss these varieties and more. Students may be given opportunities to write about how language variation is represented in popular media and how the media portray people from different cultures—in negative as well as in positive ways.

THE VALUE OF SOUTHERN LANGUAGE AND CULTURE

Reed (1982) found that, when asked where they would live if they could live anywhere they wanted, Southerners were more likely than individuals from any other part of the United States to say "right here." When asked to name the "best American state," Southerners were most likely to say their own: About 90% of North Carolinians said their state was the best, compared to less than 50% of people from Massachusetts. Furthermore, Southerners tend to want their children to go to school in the South. Reed (1982) explained:

> If expenses were no problem, only New Englanders are more likely than Southerners to name a school in their own region. (Two-thirds of the Southerners did so the last time the question was asked, despite the poor national reputation of Southern schools; only 3 percent of non-Southerners chose Southern schools.) (p. 136)

Differences between Southern values and those of the Northern educational system have contributed to the stereotype of the South as being backward or ignorant—and of Southern ways of speaking as the same. McWhiney (1988) argued that the American South is culturally distinct from the American North because the South retains a strong influence from the Celtic cultures of the Scots-Irish settlers in the 18th and 19th centuries. Celtic culture values oratory performance, which has led to the development of a strong oral tradition that has influenced Southern storytelling and preaching. The fact that Southern culture strongly values oral communication, however, should not be misinterpreted to indicate that Southerners do not also value written communication and literacy.

In the 18th and 19th centuries, schools in the South were underdeveloped. In 1880, the average Southern student attended school only 23.6 days per year, while students in the more urban, industrial Northeast attended school 72 days per year (Gershenberg, 1970). As a result, many wealthy Southern planters sent their children to be educated either in the North or abroad in England. When Northern schools tried to assimilate

Southern students, they often denigrated Southern culture by approaching it as unrefined and in need of eradication, and many Southerners resented their children returning home with anti-Southern attitudes. McWhiney (1988) reported that one Southern man rhetorically asked why Southerners should spend "their wealth . . . upon [Yankee] institutions and faculties who esteem it a condescension to teach Southern pupils and spurn their parents and guardians as graceless barbarians" (p. 201).

Even in modern culture, Southern values surrounding education may not mirror those that many Northerners might hold. As DeYoung (1995) explained with regard to Appalachia, some cultural groups may value local institutions like churches, kinship networks, and families more highly than more impersonal institutions, such as school systems. DeYoung further notes that mistrust may also arise because schooling often prepares students for careers that risk their moving away from home, outside of the region, to obtain jobs. Instead, locals may prefer that children learn how to perform skilled physical labor, which is more likely to allow them to stay and work in the area. Educators are often left to mediate between different value systems in an attempt to increase graduation and school attendance rates while still respecting the traditions and values of different cultural groups. Indeed, Southern students cannot be expected to succeed in classrooms that do not acknowledge and respect their values and worldviews (Salatino, 1995). For Southern students, negative attitudes about their culture, negative stereotypes about their abilities, and lower educational expectations for their success translate directly into fewer educational opportunities and more limited educational and occupational attainment.

Beyond cultural factors related to education, the disparity in economic resources that was present in the 18th and 19th centuries still affects education in the South. According to the Southern Educational Foundation (Suitts, 2007), in the 1800s Southern states had low per capita wealth, which translated into fewer resources for schools. Although Southern cities are now expanding and enjoying newfound prosperity, persistent social problems like high rates of underemployment and unemployment have increased the numbers of low-income households in the South, while population growth has also strained the resources of Southern states. In 2007, "for the first time in more than 40 years, the South is the only region in the nation where low income children constitute a majority of public school students" at a record-high level of 54% (Suitts, 2007, p. 2). Adding to the burdens faced by low-income students is the fact that the South generally has the lowest expenditures per K–12 pupil in the nation, and many Southern states provide very little need-based financial aid for college. The Southern Educational Foundation stresses that the South urgently needs "not only to improve but also to *transform* its public education systems" (Suitts, 2007, p. 2).

At the same time, Southern schools excel on measures of diversity. The South has the most diverse teaching force of any region in the country: Around 25% of Southern teachers are non-White, compared to around 10% nationally; and around 20% of Southern teachers are African American, compared to around 6% nationally (Frankenberg & Orfield, 2006). As the South is becoming more diverse, a similarly diverse population of educators can connect with students and help them succeed.

A Dilemma for Students

Southern students may face strong prejudices against their linguistic, cultural, and regional heritage. Purcell-Gates (1997) wrote of the special educational issues facing poor White students, especially those from Southern backgrounds: "Most people in the United States are not used to thinking about Whites as minorities or as the objects of prejudice and injustice"; however, while poor Whites have not faced discrimination based on skin color, "the literacy attainment of poor whites is significantly below that of middle-class whites, reflecting the socioeconomic status that they share with the many minorities of color" (p. 180).

Many Southern students have found that, regardless of their social class, the way they speak may make them stand out in school. Fama (2007) studied attitudes related to Southern English, especially in college settings. Fama recounts the story of a young Southerner whose professor once told her that she would always sound less intelligent than she is because of her Southern accent. This professor then suggested that the student take courses to learn how to cover it up. Students often hold the opinions of their professors in high regard and take them to heart, and the young woman quoted by Fama revealed that this professor's comment hurt her self-image and led directly to her desire to cover up her accent soon after coming to college. At the same time, the strength of language as a marker of personal and regional identity is deep. Speakers who have strived to eliminate their accents may nevertheless feel a deep cultural loss once the accents are gone.

A STUDENT'S PERSPECTIVE

"Having gone to school in North Carolina from kindergarten through college, I easily recognized Southern drawls in my fellow students; but, being the son of two Northerners in the

South, I never really felt like I had much of a Southern accent. In my sophomore year of college, I studied abroad at a private American university in Athens, Greece, with other American exchange students. Although I was the only student from the South out of about 100 students, I still felt that my 'accent' (compared to those I grew up with in North Carolina) was nonexistent and was not an issue. I became acutely aware that this was not the case when, on the first day of classes, I raised my hand and asked a question to my professor. The response I received from the class, as well as my professor, was an uncomfortable silence that lasted at least 15 seconds until a student from New York who was sitting next to me said, 'You're such a hick!' I realized then that my Southern speech was the primary lens through which I was being viewed."

The manual *Teaching for Inclusion*, published by the University of North Carolina at Chapel Hill Center for Teaching and Learning (1997), explained that regional bias in the classroom can be extremely harmful to faculty and students. The fact that UNC is a public university where most undergraduates are from North Carolina while most of the graduate students, teaching assistants, and professors are from other areas of the United States or the world

> creates a certain "class consciousness" on all sides about geographical origins. Regional accents can elicit strongly prejudiced reactions both from your students' classmates and from your teaching peers. The resulting clash of stereotypes can be quite hurtful to both teachers and students, and if they are left unchallenged, they can create unnecessary tensions in the classroom. (p. 92)

The manual provides quotes from Southern students who have experienced such regional and linguistic biases, as well as the experience of a teaching assistant at UNC who grew up in North Carolina. She struggled with the stereotypes and biases of a fellow teaching assistant from New Jersey, who often complained about and belittled Southern undergraduates in his classes.

> The first time I met him . . . he informed me that students up North were smarter and not as slack as students here in the South. . . . [He] proceeded to "warn" me that the only bright students I would have in my labs would be students from up North, and that since the majority of my students would be from North Carolina, I could expect a "general level of stupidity" from them. Throughout the semester he has continued to make comments like "as soon as I heard their accents I knew to brace myself for their stupid questions"

> and "I just make the lab as hard as I can and then wade through their stupidity and ignorance." . . . [Yet] my two labs are predominantly native North Carolinian freshmen and I have found them to be intelligent, inquisitive and hard-working. (UNC-CH, 1997, pp. 93–94)

Southerners who attend colleges and universities outside the South may also feel internal conflict over the pressure to adapt to new linguistic climates, as experienced by author bell hooks (1999), who left Kentucky to attend Stanford University.

> Coming to Stanford with my own version of a Kentucky accent I learned to speak differently while maintaining the speech of my region, the sound of my family and community. . . . In recent years, I have endeavored to use various speaking styles in the classroom as a teacher. . . . Learning to listen to different voices, hearing different speech challenges the notion that we must all assimilate—share a single, similar talk—in educational institutions. Language reflects the culture from which we emerge. (p. 79)

Attitudes, ideas, and ideologies surrounding Southern English in the classroom are complex. Students may hear prejudices about their accents, their intelligence, and their abilities expressed by other students and by faculty. Students may remain proud of their cultural and linguistic heritage, but they may also internalize these stereotypes and prejudices. These tensions may lead students to desire to "cover up" their accents or their regional backgrounds (Dyer, 1998; Wilkinson, 1999), doubt their own abilities, experience low self-esteem, and even drop out of school.

A Dilemma for Educators

Educators may also experience tension surrounding the use of Southern English. On the one hand, speaking with a Southern accent is highly valued within the South as a marker of cultural authenticity. Students and educators from the South will likely have grown up hearing and speaking Southern English. Many Southern educators also go back to teach in their home communities, where they will have Southern students and will hear Southern English being spoken. In the film *Voices of North Carolina* (Hutcheson, 2005), Cheryl Macintosh, a teacher from Atlantic, North Carolina, expressed pride in her Southern accent and her sense that a common accent allows her to relate to her students, saying, "When they told me when I started teaching that I was gonna have to change my dialect so my kids would understand me, I said, not where I'm going, I won't! 'Cause they all talk just like I do."

Educators who value Southern English as a cultural artifact and a mode of expression also know that there is often a stigma attached to Southern English, expressed in the media, by outsiders, and sometimes by Southerners themselves. Part of the dilemma for educators is the knowledge that speaking in standardized English can have many tangible benefits for their students. Educators know that students who do not sound Southern are more likely to be told that they sound educated and succeed in their educational and job experiences and less likely to be told that they sound country, redneck, ignorant, or uneducated.

Faced with this dilemma, Southern English–speaking educators might find that they vary in their own use of Southern English features with their students. Southern English–speaking educators may find themselves switching into and out of Southern English patterns with their students, modeling the ability to use features of standardized English as well as features of Southern English in different situations and with different audiences. They may also struggle with whether and how to correct features of Southern English in the writing, oral reading, and speech of their students.

There is a middle ground, however, in which Southern English speakers are taught to retain and value their Southern speech, while still learning standardized English forms and understanding when to use different language varieties. Educators best serve students when they understand the language patterns that Southern students bring with them into school situations and when they teach students to develop linguistic versatility and cultivate their interest in language (Higgs, Manning, & Miller, 1995; Salatino, 1995). Through this process, students learn to choose how best to communicate in a variety of social and educational situations.

Throughout this chapter, we provide some strategies to help educators face these dilemmas in linguistically informed ways. To aid educators in understanding the patterns of Southern English, we also present some common features that Southern English–speaking students may use in their writing, oral reading, and speech and discuss educational implications surrounding their use. Not all Southern students use all of these features. Southern students may speak Southern English to different degrees for a variety of reasons, including where in the South they come from, whether their friends and family members speak Southern English, and personal choice.

FEATURES OF SOUTHERN ENGLISH

Even though the South is broad and diverse, common elements of Southern English are found across its many varieties. These linguistic features are generally the characteristics of Southern English that are *most unlike* those of standardized English. Some features of Southern English overlap with those of other varieties of English, but many Southern features are unique.

Sound

The question of whether a person "sounds" Southern has to do with the ways that various consonant and vowel sounds, as well as other sound-related features, such as pitch and tone, function in this variety of English. Several sound-related features of Southern English have educational implications for students who use these variants.

The *r* sound. The *r* sound often varies in English; it may be absent (or partly absent, so that it sounds more like a vowel) in many English varieties. Consider how *r* sounds in the accents of speakers from New York (who may pronounce the name of their city as "New Yawk") and Boston (as in the phrase "pahk the cah" for "park the car"). In the past, *r* absence was also characteristic of the speech of Southerners. In the antebellum South, White aristocrats often sent their children to England to be educated. In British English, *r* sounds at the end of syllables (as in *four* or *fear*) had gone silent around the 17th century; this British trend was picked up by Southern elites and carried back to the South (Wolfram, 2006, p. 118). In films such as *Gone with the Wind* (Fleming, 1939), characters have the *r* absence that was found throughout most of the South during that time period.

Since that time, *r* absence has become more variable in the South. The contemporary dominant form among White Southerners is a pattern that derives from Appalachia, in which *r* sounds in words such as *mother* are always pronounced. Exceptions include language patterns found in Charleston, South Carolina (which locals pronounce "Chahlston"), among some older Southerners, and in the speech of African Americans.

***-ing* and *-in* alternation.** Throughout the United States, it is common to hear people pronouncing words that end with *-ing* as if they ended with *-in*. This process occurs when the *-ing* sound occurs in an unstressed syllable, so that words such as *running* may be pronounced as "runnin'," *walking* as "walkin'," and *eating* as "eatin'." The alternation of *-in* and *-ing* does not occur only with verbs. Nouns and adjectives ending with *-ing* can also be pronounced as *-in*, yielding such phrases as "the tall buildin'" for "the tall building" and "shoppin' cart" for *shopping cart*. This particular substitution can often be found in Southerners' speech. In this regard, the alternation of *-in* and *-ing* is a prevalent marker of Southern English, even as it is common among all American English speakers.

"*Wadn't*" and *wasn't* alternation. Speakers of Southern English tend to pronounce the *z* sound as a *d* sound before nasal consonants (the *m, n,* and *ng* sounds), especially in contraction words. Thus, words such as *isn't, wasn't,* and *doesn't* may be pronounced as "idn't," "wadn't," and "dudn't." Other words that have a *z* sound followed by a nasal sound also follow this pattern, including *business,* which may be pronounced as "bidness."

The *ai* sound. Vowel patterns often make Southern English stand out, and vowels are one of the hardest features for a person to shift or change in their own speech. One of the most recognizable and often most stigmatized vowel features of Southern English is Southerners' merging of the *ah* and *ai* sounds. Thus, the word *time* may be pronounced as "tom," *bye* may be pronounced as "bah," *died* may be pronounced as "dad," and *mile* may be pronounced as "mall." In addition, words such as *tire* may be pronounced as "tar," and *fire* may be pronounced as "far." Merging of the *ah* and *ai* sounds is common in Southern English, regardless of racial or ethnic background, age, gender, or social class.

The *oy* sound. The *oy* sound in Southern speech may also differ from how this vowel is pronounced in standardized English. Among many Southerners, the *oy* sound may be pronounced as "oh" when it occurs before *l*. Thus, *oil* may be pronounced as "oll" or "all," *boil* may be pronounced as "boll" or "ball," and *toil* may be pronounced as "toll" or "tall."

The "pin"–"pen" merger. Southern English speakers may pronounce lax (or sometimes called "short") *i* and *e* vowel sounds in similar ways when they appear before the nasal sounds *n, m,* and *ng*. For example, *pen* may be pronounced as "pin," *ten* may be pronounced as "tin," *hem* may be pronounced as "him," and *Jenny* may be pronounced as "Ginny."

The "fill"–"feel" and "fail"–"fell" mergers. In Southern English, words such as *feel* may be pronounced as "feel" or as "fill," but *fill* may also be pronounced as "fill" or as "feel." *Heel* may be pronounced as "heel" or as "hill," but *hill* may also be pronounced as "hill" or as "heel," and so forth. Similarly, in Southern English, words such as *fail* may be pronounced as "fail" or as "fell," *hail* may be pronounced as "hail" or as "hell," and *bail* may be pronounced as "bail" or as "bell."

The *ant* sound. In Southern English, *ain't, can't,* and *aunt* may all sound as though they have exactly the same vowel. In general, many English speakers have trouble telling whether a speaker of standardized English is saying *can* or *can't* and often have to ask, "Did you say *can* or *can't*?" The innovative Southern English pronunciation of *can't* as "kain't" makes the word *can't* more distinguishable to the ear as being the negative form of *can*. Much as *can't* may be pronounced as "kain't" in the South, the word *aunt* may also be pronounced as "ain't." In most of the United States, *aunt* may be pronounced in two ways: either "ant" or "ahnt" (rhyming with *font*). In the South, however, speakers have the option of pronouncing *aunt* in three ways: as "ant," as "ahnt," and as "ain't."

Educational implications. There are specific educational implications for students who have these Southern sound features in their speech. For one, Southern English–speaking students may have very different notions of which words rhyme, due to their vowel variation, than their non-Southern counterparts. Southern English–speaking students may think of *pen* and *pin, Ben* and *bin, den* and *din* as rhyming words, due to the so-called "pen"–"pin" merger in their speech. Because words such as *pen* and *pin, time* and *Tom,* and *wheel* and *will* may be pronounced the same, Southern English–speaking students may also spell these words the same in their essays and papers. For example, younger Southern English–speaking students, who may be just learning the connection between sounds and letters, may spell *friend* "fran" or "frind." *Went* may be spelled "wint," *them* may be spelled "thim," *when* may be spelled "whin" or "win," *meant* may be spelled "mint," and *Wednesday* may be spelled "winsday." Older Southern English–speaking students may have similar challenges with new and/or unfamiliar words. They might spell *since* as "sense" and vice versa. They may also have trouble distinguishing *wince* from *whence* or may spell *lamenting* as "laminting." The words *eminent* and *imminent,* which to most Southern English–speaking students sound the same, may also be similarly difficult. A word such as *repeal* may also, due to vowel mergers, be spelled "repill," and a word such as *travail* may be spelled "travel" or "travell."

It is critical to be able to determine what are actual errors of understanding in students' writing and what are errors based on language variation. To distinguish between actual errors and language variations, it is helpful to take into account the context of what the student is saying. For example, if a Southern English–speaking student spells "frind" when context clues suggest that the student means *friend* or spells "since" when it appears that the student means *sense,* then, in all likelihood, the spelling mistake is not a haphazard one but is rather a result of Southern English speakers' tendency to pronounce the *i* and *e* vowels in words such as *pen* and *pin* the same way.

When assessing standardized speech or writing, before marking student mistakes, it is thus necessary to consider whether the potential error might be rooted in language variation. By consulting the linguistic features that we discuss in this book, educators may be able to discern whether the perceived errors appear to fit a linguistic pattern characteristic of Southern English. If they do, it is important to explain to the student the linguistic pattern. This process entails pointing out to the student their Southern English–influenced pattern and, while acknowledging and appreciating this language variation, revealing to the student how this pattern compares and contrasts with that of standardized English.

Grammar

Grammatical features of Southern English may be more noticeable and stigmatized than sound-related features. It is important to remember that regardless of the greater stigmatization of Southern English grammatical features, they are just as systematic, regular, and patterned as other language variants, including variants that characterize standardized English.

Ain't. The word *ain't* is often used as a helping or linking verb in nonstandardized varieties of English. Many speakers of English, including Southern English speakers, use *ain't* instead of *am not, isn't,* and *aren't,* as in sentences such as "I ain't hungry," "He ain't old enough," and "We ain't going home yet." In addition, many Southern English speakers use *ain't* instead of *hasn't* and *haven't,* as in sentences such as "I ain't seen her." Southern English speakers also commonly use *ain't* for emphasis or effect.

Multiple negatives. While the use of multiple negatives within one sentence or clause is highly stigmatized, they are not uncommon in Southern English or in other nonstandardized varieties of English. Sentences such as "He don't know nothing," "I ain't seen him neither," and "She ain't here no more" can be uttered by speakers throughout the United States. Multiple negatives are also found in many languages of the world, including Spanish, French, Russian, Czech, Polish, Greek, Hungarian, Hebrew, and Japanese. Multiple negatives were much more prevalent in older varieties of English than they are in today's variety of standardized English. Chaucer, for example, often used double and triple negatives in his poetry. Contrary to the claim often made that "double negatives cancel each other out in English," the meanings of English sentences that contain multiple negatives are generally quite clear.

In the South, multiple negatives can be formed and used in unique ways. Among Southern English speakers, it is possible to invert the verb and the negative marker, as in sentences such as "Can't nobody hear nothing in this crowded room" (in standardized English, "Nobody can hear anything in this crowded room") and "Ain't nothing you can do to fix that car" (in standardized English, "You can't do anything to fix that car"). It is also possible for Southern speakers to carry negative markers throughout multiple clauses in a sentence, as in "She wasn't convinced that he wasn't doing nothing" (or, in standardized English, "She wasn't convinced that he wasn't doing anything").

Southern English speakers also use multiple negation with negative adverbs such as *barely, scarcely,* and *hardly,* which are often used to add emphasis to statements. Sentences such as "I can't hardly never hear what she's saying" and "I can't scarcely figure him out" are common in the South. To a Southerner, the sentence "I can't hardly never hear what she's saying" may express a much more emphatic claim than the standardized English sentence "I can hardly hear what she's saying."

STRATEGIES FOR EDUCATORS

Using the terms *School English* and *Southern English* may be helpful in introducing students to the idea of language variation without demeaning the language that students bring with them from home. Higgs and colleagues (1995) found that Appalachian children, by second or third grade, had already picked up on differences between language patterns used at home versus those used at school. Educators may extend students' linguistic awareness by guiding students to compare and contrast the specific features of Southern English and standardized English in ways that value both varieties. In so doing, educators help students develop their linguistic versatility and confidence. (Higgs et al., 1995; Salatino, 1995)

Absence of plural markers. In Southern English, speakers generally pluralize regular nouns the same way as it is done in standardized English: by adding an *-s* to the end of the noun (as in "two cat*s*," "six dog*s*," and "three house*s*"). In Southern English, however, for nouns of weight or measure, such as the words *pound* and *mile,* the plural marker is optional, particularly when used with numbers. As a result, phrases such as "four pound," "twenty mile," "fifty cent," "three foot," and "six ton" are common.

STRATEGIES FOR EDUCATORS

In order to foster language awareness, students can be encouraged to keep personal language diaries to record how they speak and write. Andrews (2006) described an exercise for a language diary, in which students carry a journal and record the phrases, words, and sounds that represent the language variety they use. For example, students may record that they typically say sentences such as "He weighs 200 pound," or "The road is three mile long." Journal entries may be used to help students develop a personalized checklist to consult when they are producing compositions in standardized English. For example, students may check to make sure that all regular plural nouns of weight or measure have an *-s* on them, as in "He weighs 200 pounds" and "The road is three miles long."

Regularization of pronouns and possessives. The use of nonstandardized English pronouns such as *hisself* and *theirself* and nonstandardized English possessives like *yourn* and *hisn* may be marked as a serious error in standardized English. These features occur for reasons related to regularization, which is the linguistic tendency to make grammatical patterns more uniform. For example, consider the standardized English pronoun forms *myself, herself, yourselves,* and *ourselves.* Southern English speakers may regularize this pattern, yielding the following paradigm: *myself, yourself, hisself, herself, ourself, yourself,* and *theirself* or *theirselves.* In much the same way, possessives like *yourn* and *hisn* are produced when Southern English speakers regularize inconsistencies within the standardized English pattern for marking possession. Just as *mine* ends in an *n* sound, words such as *yourn, hisn, hern,* and *ourn* similarly came about to signal possession. Thus, Southern English speakers may produce sentences such as "This one's my book, and that one's yourn."

Regularization of verb patterns. Many nonstandardized verb forms that are used in Southern English are products of the ways that Southern English, and other varieties of English, pattern differently from standardized English. For example, the standardized English phrase "I saw her" may be produced by Southern speakers as "I seen her," "I seened her," or "I seed her." Southern English speakers may also alternate the verb forms *was* and *wasn't* with *were* and *weren't,* as in sentences such as "The children was laughing for hours" and "They wasn't there." They may also alternate the verb forms *is* and *isn't* with *are* and *aren't,* as in sentences such as "The eggs is cracked" and "Those cars isn't fixed yet." In these and similar sentences, nonstandardized forms, including *is* for *are*, are not haphazard errors in subject–verb agreement but instead are patterned language variations. These and other nonstandardized verb patterns have long and well-established histories. For instance, the use of *is* with the subject *you*, as in "You is at home," has been documented as a feature of English from the 1600s (Wallace, 2001).

Generally speaking, there are four different patterns for how verbs vary in nonstandardized varieties of English. Verbs that are irregular in standardized English may be made more uniform in their patterning. For example, instead of following the standardized verb paradigm *I wasn't, you weren't, he/she/it wasn't, we weren't, you weren't, they weren't*, speakers of Southern English and other nonstandardized English varieties may make the pattern more uniform by using *wasn't* for *weren't*, yielding *I wasn't, you wasn't, he/she/it wasn't, we wasn't, you wasn't, they wasn't*. In some areas of the country, such as on the Outer Banks of North Carolina (as well as in many parts of England), speakers may adopt a different pattern, whereby they regularize all the *was/were* verbs to *weren't*: Instead of *I wasn't, you wasn't*, and so on, these speakers are more likely to say *I weren't, you weren't, he/she/it weren't*, and so on.

STRATEGIES FOR EDUCATORS

Educators can explicitly instruct students on the patterns of verb conjugation in standardized English while acknowledging differences in the verb patterns that may exist in students' home varieties. In doing so, care should be taken to avoid statements such as "Don't use *was* when you should use *were*," which may be taken as a rebuke, or "Make sure your subjects and verbs agree," which may be unclear.

Instead, it is important for students to be aware of variations in language patterns. For example, educators can guide students using such questions as "In School English, what is the pattern for using *was* versus *were*?" It is critical to talk about "different patterns" rather than "correct" and "incorrect" English.

Above all, it is important not to take a correctionist attitude toward Southern English, whereby students' language variants are marked across the board as "errors," but rather to model for students the specific features they are expected to learn and use. If students are unsure why they are getting marked down, correction may backfire. Students who are critiqued without sufficient explanation may become overwhelmed, confused, and discouraged. They may also lose confidence in the learning process, in their own abilities, in their educators, and even in school. (Labov, 1995)

Speakers of Southern English and other varieties of English may also regularize verb patterns by using a regular verb ending on irregular verbs. Most verbs in English simply mark the past tense by adding *-ed,* as with the verbs *walked, talked, marked, banned,* and *pushed.* For some verbs, however, standardized English calls for irregular past tenses; for example, *know* becomes *knew, run* becomes *ran,* and *bring* becomes *brought.* Southern English speakers (and speakers of many varieties of English) may take these irregular verb forms and make them regular by using *-ed* endings, thereby eliminating the irregularity. Thus, Southern English speakers might say *knowed* instead of *knew, runned* instead of *ran,* and *bringed* instead of *brought.* Such forms, while considered nonstandardized, actually adhere more to the dominant pattern of how English verbs are changed into the past tense. The tendency toward regularization is a common process in how English verbs have changed over time. Furthermore, in many cases, irregular older forms have become regularized in today's standardized English. Whereas speakers of older forms of English used the verb forms *besought, throve,* and *holp,* for example, speakers today use *beseeched, thrived,* and *helped.*

Speakers of Southern English, and of other varieties of English, may also use the bare root form of a verb, with no past tense endings, if the past tense is otherwise clear. In sentences such as "He come to work in a T-shirt last week" and "They give their kids better presents last year," the phrases "last week" and "last year" already mark that the event in question occurred in the past. Practically speaking, it can be seen as redundant to mark the sentence as being in the past through the use of both a past tense verb form (e.g., *came, gave*) and another past tense marker (e.g., *last week, last year*). To resolve this redundancy, Southern English speakers may use a present tense verb form (e.g., *come, give*) with a past tense marker (e.g., *last week, last year*). In doing so, they regularize the verb form while still signaling that the event in question occurred in the past.

In addition, some Southern English speakers may occasionally use past tense verb forms that have become archaic in standardized English, as in such sentences as "I hearn [heard] something behind me" and "Something just riz [rose] up right before my eyes." These types of forms are retentions and adaptations of older forms of English that have been preserved in the South.

Multiple modal verbs. Verbs such as *can, could, should, shall, would, will, may, might,* and *must* are called modal verbs; in standardized English generally only one modal verb is used in a given verb phrase. In Southern English, it is possible to use two or even three modal verbs together. These combinations, called double modals or multiple modals, often carry specialized meanings related to permission and mobility that the use of single modal verbs in standardized English cannot impart. Multiple modals are prevalent in Scotland, northern Britain, and Northern Ireland, as well as in the West Indies and the Caribbean. They are also found in the Gullah language and African American English.

Mishoe and Montgomery (1994) found that Southern English speakers frequently use multiple modals, regardless of gender, race and ethnicity, and social class. The most common combinations of modal verbs are *might can, might could, might would,* and *used to would.* A Southerner might say sentences such as "I *might can* pick you up after school, if I have time," "I *might could* go to the party, if I can find a ride," "I *might would* want a new bicycle for Christmas, depending on how much it costs," and "We *used to would* go running every day after school, but we don't anymore." The use of multiple modal verbs in these sentences adds nuance to the conditions surrounding the potential event that may occur.

Multiple modals also often occur in face-to-face interaction as part of strategies of being polite, for example, in "negotiations, when one person attempts to resolve an issue or question by seeking action, agreement, information, or approval from another person" (Mishoe & Montgomery, 1994, p. 14). In these cases, Southern English speakers commonly use multiple modals to add extra mitigation and indirectness to a request they are making of another person. For example, a speaker might say, "I'll tell you what we might should better do," instead of "I'll tell you what we should do," to mitigate the statement, and a student might ask an instructor, "We were wondering if we might could get a copy of last year's test" as a way to sound more polite than asking "can we" or "could we."

Fixin' to. The use of *fixin' to* (also pronounced "fixta" or "finna") can be used by Southern English speakers to indicate immediate future action, as in "It looks like it's fixin' to rain" and "I'm fixin' to go to the store, as soon as I find my purse." Whereas standardized English might use *about to, getting ready to,* or *planning to,* Southern English speakers use *fixin' to* to convey a sense of immediacy or impending action.

STRATEGIES FOR EDUCATORS

Southern English–speaking students may be encouraged to find examples of ways they talk that may vary according to social context or audience. For example, students may discuss when they would use a sentence such as "I'm fixin' to move my car" compared to "I'm getting ready to move my car." Such strategies attune students' ears to language variation while sending the message that school is a place for learning, curiosity, expansion, and exploration.

Done. The word *done* may be used in a unique way among speakers of Southern English to mark a completed action in the past tense. In sentences such as "I done told you where he went" and "He done met my mother, but this was his first time meeting my father," the action being referred to was already completed some time ago. Sometimes *done* can add emphasis or intensity to a statement, and sometimes a speaker may be implying that the hearer should already have known that this action had been completed. Thus, if a student tells a teacher, "I done finished my homework," the student is likely saying that not only did she finish her homework, but she finished it a long time ago.

***a-* prefixing.** Particularly in Appalachia, speakers may attach an *a-* prefix (pronounced "uh") to different words. Most commonly, this feature occurs with verb forms ending in *-ing*, but it occasionally occurs with other types of words, such as adjectives and adverbs. Sentences such as "The old dog was up there just a-panting, his tongue a-hanging out," "They ran a-backwards and forwards," and "I went a-swimming in the river once when I was young" might be heard among Southern English speakers.

Educational implications. For Southern English–speaking students, using nonstandardized grammatical forms in their speech or writing can have unintended educational consequences. For example, whereas multiple negatives are used in many varieties of English, Southern English is more apt to use multiple negatives that include negative adverbs, such as *scarcely*, *barely*, and *hardly*, and these adverbs are often used for emphasis. As a result, Southern English–speaking students may think of these words as carrying an emphatic meaning, not a negative one. Thus, Southern English–speaking students may not be able to easily spot where the use of negative adverbs in their speech or writing creates a "double negative" situation in standardized English.

If Southern English–speaking students produce sentences such as "I can't hardly hear what she's saying," they may need explicit instruction to understand that words such as *hardly* "count" as negative words, and thus they have produced a double negative. When Christine gave presentations to junior and senior English majors at several Southern universities, the students said that being explicitly taught about negative adverbs would be very helpful to those who would be taking standardized tests, including the Scholastic Aptitude Test (SAT) and the Graduate Record Exam (GRE).

Knowledge of how and why specific language variants appear in Southern English–speaking students' speech and writing is also invaluable information for educators when assessing students. When educators assess students' work, it is important to consider whether there is a possibility that potential errors might actually be rooted in the students' knowledge of Southern English. First, educators may discern whether the perceived error fits a linguistic pattern characteristic of Southern English. If so, it is critical not to mark an error as "wrong" and move on, but rather to explain the patterns underlying the mistake, a process that entails showing students the details of their Southern English–influenced usage patterns and comparing them to the usage patterns that characterize standardized English.

If a student is using many features of Southern English in her or his writing, it may be useful to allow that student to talk about how features of the home language variety enable the student's communication and expression. For example, if a student frequently uses multiple modal verbs in essays, consider talking to her or him in a one-on-one meeting about this feature. The student may communicate the fact that multiple modals can have specialized meanings in Southern English that they do not have in standardized English. The educator can affirm these insights while also suggesting strategies for how to approximate the meaning of multiple modals in situations that call for the use of standardized English verb forms.

Without guidance, it is difficult for students to know any exact strategies for addressing language variations in their writing, oral reading, and/or speaking. In a presentation that Christine gave at a university in South Carolina, one young man spoke up. He shared that he had been to the writing center on campus many times for help with his writing. As he spoke with a look of shame, he related that he could not figure out how to write "right" and that his writing did not sound like it was "supposed to" but that he did not know how to fix it. Educators who are well versed in the features of Southern English will be able to point out to struggling Southern English–speaking students where language variations arise in their writing, oral reading, and/or speaking and where students might need to make accommodations in situations that call for the use of standardized English.

Pitch, Tone, Rhythm, and Volume

The melodic aspects of language, including pitch, tone, rhythm, and volume, reflect important characteristics about a given speaker or what a speaker is communicating. Melodic features may give a sense of whether a speaker is asking a question or making a statement; they may give listeners clues about a speaker's emotional state; and they may give listeners clues as to how to interpret what a speaker is saying—for example, whether or not someone is being sarcastic, ironic, suggestive, or playful. These features are also important in educational situations because educators and students frequently rely on melodic cues when they interact and interpret each other's styles of communication.

Rate of speech. According to Preston (1998), the perception that Southerners talk more slowly than other speakers is a popular stereotype that has some truth to it. Salmons, Jacewicz, and Fox (2008) analyzed the ways that 40 speakers from south central Wisconsin and 40 speakers from western North Carolina read 240 different sentences out loud. On average, the Wisconsiners spoke at a rate of 3.8 syllables per second, and the North Carolinians spoke at a rate of 3.4 syllables per second. Statistically speaking, the Wisconsiners read their sentences out loud faster than the North Carolinians did. In part, Salmons and colleagues (2008) explain, Southerners' slower rate of talking is largely due to two factors. First, Southern English speakers' vowels are, on average, longer than both Northern speakers' vowels and Midwestern speakers' vowels (which are, on average, longer than Northern speakers' vowels). Second, Southern English speakers sometimes produce what in standardized English are single vowel sounds, known as monophthongs, as double vowel sounds, known as diphthongs (e.g., pronouncing *field* as "fee-yuld" or *bed* as "bay-ud"). These lengthened vowels often add up, leading Southerners to take slightly longer to pronounce what they are saying.

Syllable stress. In Southern English, the stress on words can differ from the stress patterns of standardized English. In some words for which speakers of standardized English place stress on the second syllable, Southern English speakers can place the stress on the first syllable. For example, the word *umbrella,* generally pronounced as "um-BRELL-a" by speakers of standardized English, can be pronounced as "UM-brell-a" in Southern English; *insurance,* pronounced as "in-SUR-ance" in standardized English, can be pronounced as "IN-sur-ance" in Southern English; and *police,* pronounced as "po-LICE" in standardized English, can be pronounced as "PO-lice" in Southern English.

Conversation

Conversational norms in the South can differ from those in other regions of the United States. Conversations among Southerners more often begin with different types of pleasantries than they do elsewhere in the country; Southern conversations also often start with "hey," whereas other Americans might say "hi" or "hello." One small college in the South held a "hey day" on the first day of classes. Northern students were confused, wondering why a college would sponsor a "hay" day, but the point was to get students to greet each other by saying "hey."

STRATEGIES FOR EDUCATORS

Purcell-Gates (1997) found that teaching students to recognize differences in greetings and other conversational conventions increases students' awareness of differences across Southern English, African American English, and standardized English without devaluing any language variety. Educators can discuss what to say when meeting another person (e.g., "Pleased to meet you," "It's very nice to meet you") or what to say in other situations that may arise. This type of explicit instruction may be extended to other features, such as vocabulary items and writing conventions, as educators provide students with such guidance as "When you write a letter, begin with 'Dear So-and-So.'"

In conversations, Southerners often ask each other how they are doing, often more than once. They may ask questions such as how the other person's family members are doing and how their job is going before they get down to business with the actual reason for chatting. To Southerners, making small talk is a necessary part of being polite, and Southern English speakers may feel that people who jump right into a conversation seem pushy or rushed.

Southern English speakers also use the phrase "I tell you what" more often in conversation. Koops (2006) found that Southerners are more likely to produce sentences such as "I tell you what, would you like to swap e-mails and maybe chat sometime" and "That guy is bad news, I tell you what." These and other linguistic variations give a Southern flavor to speakers' conversations and may also appear in Southern English–speaking students' speech and writing.

Storytelling. Southerners have a reputation for being great orators and storytellers. From the famous Uncle Remus stories to the Jack tales found in Appalachian culture, many stories that have been printed in books were first told orally. Other traditions that center on language in Southern speech and music include the Hollerin' Contest in North Carolina, in which contestants practice *hollerin'*, a practice that emerged as a way for rural people to communicate across long distances (Hartman, 2000). Southerners have also built a rich tradition of storytelling through music, as seen in the lyrics of bluegrass or country music and of Appalachian folk music, represented in films such as *Songcatcher* (Greenwald, 2000).

STRATEGIES FOR EDUCATORS

The examination of multiple literacy practices in Southern culture may help to teach all students about language diversity. Educators can hold storytelling or poetry workshops, and guest speakers may read, recite poetry, or tell stories in Southern English. Students may compose their own work, modeled after what they have heard. Younger students may be interested in storytelling, while advanced students may examine rhetorical style in Southern novels, songs, and sermons. Older students may also listen to different speeches by Southern orators, examining how these speakers use features of standardized English and of Southern English and considering what social and personal reasons might have led these speakers to develop their rhetorical styles.

All students may be encouraged to read a variety of different texts and talk about the language variation they find in them. Goodman (2003) recommended an exercise in which students practice group oral readings of texts that are written in different varieties of English. Younger students may enjoy reading stories that use Southern English and Appalachian English in dialogue, while older students may read novels by Southern authors such as William Faulkner and Flannery O'Connor.

Indirect speech. Southerners are often viewed as being indirect in conversation, which, in many ways, is linked to perceptions of politeness. Southerners may find direct requests to be jarring or rude. As a result, Southern English speakers may go out of their way to formulate indirect requests that include many hedges or mitigations, often because they do not want to burden another person. In the sentence "If you're sure it's not too much trouble, I'll see if you're home tonight and maybe I can borrow that dish I asked you about," words such as *maybe* and *can* and the phrase "if you're sure it's not too much trouble" soften the directness of the request and, in part, allow the other person more freedom to say no.

Indirect speech can also be easily misunderstood. For example, confusion may exist over following directions, which is usually the most important rule in a given school or classroom, beginning in preschool. Southern students' feelings may be hurt by the use of direct requests or commands that sound as though they are rebukes. Southern students who are asking for something in an indirect way may also be told to "just spit it out" or "get to the point," even though they are making their request in a ritualized way that is comfortable for them, given their Southern culture and upbringing.

Reed (1993) affirmed that what Southerners see as "manners" can often seem confusing, misleading, or even deceptive to non-Southerners. He wrote about a college student from Illinois who found Southerners' cordial greetings to each other to manifest a "superficial friendliness," whereas a student from Boston found Southerners to be sometimes friendly and sometimes just polite. Reed stated, "That would sound familiar to the Japanese, by the way. They're polite too, and they get called 'inscrutable'" (p. 127). As these opinions reveal, conversational practices can evoke strong emotions, even negative judgments, among people who do not share the same cultural and linguistic norms.

Honorifics. The use of *ma'am* and *sir* is much more common in the South than elsewhere in the United States, where calling adults *ma'am* and *sir* can be taken as being disrespectful or cheeky. In the South, the terms convey just the opposite. Johnson (2008) reported that when two English 101 classes at a university in South Carolina were surveyed, data showed that Southern English speakers used *ma'am* and *sir* for three reasons: to address someone older or in an authority position, to show respect, or to maintain or reestablish good relations with someone. *Ma'am* and *sir* are also frequently used by Southerners who work in customer service, such as restaurant servers. Wolfson and Manes (1980) found that *ma'am* and *sir* were used around 80% of the time in service interactions in the South but only about 25% of the time in the Northeast.

In some Southern families, children are taught to address their parents as *ma'am* and *sir*. Other Southern children may not use these terms with parents, but they may be expected to use them with other adults, including educators. Many educators from the South will expect their students to use *ma'am* and *sir* regularly. A Southern child who answers an adult's question with a simple "Yes" may hear the adult respond with "Yes, what?" until "Yes, ma'am" or "Yes, sir" is produced. In comparison, non-Southern educators, who may consider *ma'am* and *sir* to be strange or even offensive terms, should remember to be tolerant when they hear Southern students using them at school and explain to the student their personal preference for what to be called.

Naming practices. Southerners often employ what may appear to be unconventional naming practices. One Southern naming practice is the use of "double names," like Mary Sue, Mary Beth, Billy Bob, and Willie Joe (Reed, 1982). Southerners also often use nicknames, and they frequently call boys and men by nicknames that refer to the suffix of their name. In the South, for example, Joe Smith Jr. might be called "Junior" or "Joe Junior," whereas Joe Smith III might be called "Trey." Other family terms in the South may differ from those used in the rest of the country. Southern kinship terms include *bubba* for *brother*, *sissy* for *sister*, and *mama* and *daddy* for *mother* and *father* or *mom* and *dad* (Marin, 2002).

Southerners also might have unique terms of address for their grandparents. Names like *Meemaw* (pronounced "MEE-maw") and *Peepaw* (pronounced "PEE-paw") and *Mamaw* (pronounced "MA'AM-maw") and *Papaw* (pronounced "PAP-paw") are more common in the South than elsewhere in the United States. Kinship terms may indicate how close the bond is between grandchild and grandparent. Some speakers may call a grandmother with whom they are very close by the nickname *Meemaw*, whereas a grandmother with whom they are not very close might be called by a much more formal term, such as *Grandmother* (Marin, 2002).

Vocabulary

Some vocabulary items used in Southern English differ from vocabulary used in other parts of the United States. For example, Southern English speakers tend to refer to carbonated beverages as *Coke* far more often than speakers from other parts of the United States, who are far more likely to use *soda* or *pop* (McConchie, n.d.). Southern English speakers may also use words such as *plumb* to mean "completely" (as in "She went plumb deaf"), *slam* to mean "completely" (as in "The bullet went slam through"), *right smart* to mean "very" or "a good deal of" (as in "He's got a right smart temper"), and *reckon* to mean "think" or "believe" (as in "I reckon you're right"). Other common Southern English vocabulary items include *cut off* for "turn off" (as in "Would you cut off the lights") and "mash" for *press* (as in "Mash that button").

STRATEGIES FOR EDUCATORS

One exercise for building awareness of variation in vocabulary is to have students interview other Southern English speakers. Andrews (2006) suggested that educators encourage students of all ages to learn about how different words are used in parts of the United States to refer to the same item. Activities include having students investigate regional variation in the words that they, their family members, and their friends use. For example, students can poll others' answers to the question "Where do you get water from?" by choosing *tap, faucet,* or *spigot*. These kinds of activities benefit all students in the classroom, not just Southern English speakers. Such exercises introduce more standardized English–speaking students to the ideas of language variation, and they may spark conversations between students who come from different regional backgrounds about the fact that there is often more than one way in English to say the same thing.

Similarly, Wolfram (2000) suggested that students conduct community surveys about variation in vocabulary items. As a class, students can brainstorm a list of words that they know people use in different ways (e.g., *soft drink, shopping cart*) and then interview a range of community members about these features. Students can then tally responses, create a chart, and analyze what kinds of trends they see in the use of the words. Students may consider questions such as: What does the survey show about the language use of different groups of people? In what ways does the community dialect seem to be changing?

Andrews (2006) suggested that students conduct an interview with an older person about language use. Students may ask questions about words or phrases that the older person once heard his or her parents or grandparents use, words or phrases that the older person uses him- or herself, and how the older person feels about the language used by young people today. These activities build students' awareness of language variation and language change over time.

Perhaps no one term embodies the South quite like the word *y'all*. According to most traditional grammar books, in order to address a group of people, a speaker should say *you*. Yet the use of *you* can be confusing, since in English (unlike many other languages) the same pronoun *you* can be singular or plural. If a speaker asks a group of people at a party, "What time do you want to leave," no doubt someone will ask in return, "Do you mean all of us, or just me?" In many regions of the United States, speakers have gotten around *you* confusion by using words that specifically mean the plural *you*. Speakers across the United States often say *you guys*. In the Northeast, speakers often say *youse guys*; in Pittsburgh, Pennsylvania, speakers often say *yinz*; and in Appalachia, speakers often say *you'ns*.

Throughout most of the South, people say *y'all*. While the use of *you guys* is spreading *into* the South, the use of *y'all* is also spreading *out* to other regions of the United States. Tillery, Wikle, and Bailey (2000) found that almost 50% of non-Southerners reported using *y'all*, compared to around 85% of Southerners. As they noted, *y'all* is now a widespread term.

Montgomery (1992) investigated the many meanings and uses of *y'all* in the South. Sometimes Southerners use *y'all* to refer to just one person. Sometimes *y'all* is used when speaking to one person in order to include other people who aren't present; for example, the sentence "What are y'all doing for Thanksgiving this year?" could be asked of a single person to refer to the person's whole family. Sometimes *y'all* can refer to the institution or business that a person represents, as in the question "Do y'all sell magazines here?" when asked of a shopkeeper. *Y'all* can also be made possessive, as in the sentences "I could use y'all's help around here" and "Where did y'all's shoes go?" *Y'all* can even be made more noticeably plural by using the term *all of y'all* (pronounced "ALL-uh-yall") to ensure that listeners know the speaker is referring to an entire group, not just to one person.

When Christine gave a lecture on Southern English at a Southern university, in attendance was a teacher from New York who spoke with a strong New York accent. After the lecture he said that, while he uses *youse guys* frequently in the classroom, he nevertheless feels uncomfortable when his students use the word *y'all*. As this example illustrates, those who are unfamiliar with Southern ways of speaking may struggle with appreciating and accepting the speech patterns they hear around them.

THE TAKE-AWAY MESSAGE

Understanding language variation among Southern English–speaking students is critically important for educators in the South. Linguistically informed educators have a greater appreciation for their Southern English–speaking students' rich linguistic heritage and cultural background, and they are better equipped to instruct Southern English–speaking students in ways that enable them to value their home language patterns while mastering standardized English.

More linguistic and educational research is necessary to fully examine the linguistic and educational experiences of a growing, diverse population of Southern English–speaking students. We are working with educators to develop a broader repertoire of pedagogically sound and linguistically informed strategies for addressing variation in the oral reading, writing, and speech of Southern English–speaking students. As linguists and educators continue to work together, we are able to better foster the educational attainment of Southern English–speaking students and advance our knowledge about the nature of language variation and change in Southern American classrooms.

4

African American English: An Ethnic and Cultural Variety

African American English has been called by many names. Some terms, such as *Black English, African American English,* and *African American Vernacular English,* are more academic in origin. Other terms, including *Ebonics,* have been popularized by the media. African American English patterns have also been called *Urban English* (especially in the North and Northeast) and *Rural English* (especially in the South). In some regions of the United States, the linguistic patterns of African American speakers from a given geographic area overlap with those of speakers of other races and ethnic groups who live there as well (Paris, 2009). The sheer variety of the terms that refer to African American English illustrates the difficulty that people have had putting one name and one face on African American people and their patterns of communication.

DISCUSSION: WHAT'S IN A NAME?

Consider the many terms that have been used to refer to the linguistic patterns of Americans of African descent. Which terms have you heard? When do you think some of them might have been in use? What are some pros and cons of using the different terms?

In this chapter, we provide educators with knowledge about African American English as an ethnic and cultural variety. With this knowledge, educators can better understand their African American

English–speaking students' patterns of communication. Equipped with linguistic information and cultural sensitivity, educators can help African American English–speaking students navigate between specific African American English forms and meanings and standardized English forms and meanings. Linguistically informed educators are able to identify which features of students' speech and writing are related to African American English and which features may be evidence of reading comprehension, spelling, or writing mistakes, or even evidence of a language disorder. As a result, educators feel more empowered to identify and address specific linguistic challenges that African American English–speaking students may face.

THE HISTORY OF AFRICAN AMERICAN ENGLISH

We use the term *African American English* to refer to varieties of English used in places where African Americans live or historically have lived. Three of the most important findings about African American English are that it is spoken by millions of Americans throughout the United States, it has its roots in African languages, and it is not substandard English but rather is as systematic, rule-governed, and patterned as all other languages and language varieties.

African American English has a long history, and many of its linguistic characteristics can be traced to West African languages. There are different hypotheses as to the origin of African American English (Wolfram & Thomas, 2002). The Creolist hypothesis holds that Creole languages were formed when speakers of African languages came into contact with speakers of English in the United States and that African American English slowly formed out of Creole and English contact. In areas where speakers of African languages were more isolated, Creole languages such as Gullah, Jamaican English, and Patois still survive. Ultimately, theories on the origin of African American English remain difficult to verify, due both to the brutal nature of slavery, since speakers of similar African languages were intentionally separated, and to the lack of extensive documentation of spoken and written language patterns.

From the beginning of the European colonial presence in North America, captive Africans were brought to work the land as slaves. As Harper (2003) notes, slavery extended into the Northeast, even into New England. It was concentrated, however, in the region of the United States that is considered to be the Deep South, which includes South Carolina, Georgia, Alabama, Mississippi, and Louisiana. In 1863 the Emancipation

Proclamation was signed, and in 1865 the Thirteenth Amendment to the Constitution, which abolished slavery, was ratified.

As industry grew in the North, African Americans left the South to seek better jobs and lives outside of the confines of the segregated South and to flee lynching, race riots, and other brutal effects of Jim Crow racism. This population shift, known as the Great Migration, had a linguistic effect. As African Americans moved from more rural and racially segregated areas in the South to urban areas in the North, where they tended to live in concentrated areas, they brought their language patterns with them. Elements of Southern English merged with Northern speech patterns: Some of the features of African American English, such as the use of *y'all* or the near-identical pronunciation of words such as *pen* and *pin,* reveal that this language variety has Southern roots. Over time, this new variety of African American English spread from the cities of the Northeast to the West. It also spread back into the South, as some African Americans who had moved away from the South kept in contact with their Southern family members, while other African Americans repatriated, moving from the North back to the South.

Today, African American English is widely spoken across the United States, from large cities to rural locales. Most African Americans use features of African American English to some extent (as, sometimes, do speakers from other cultural groups and ethnic backgrounds). Patterns of residential segregation, established over time throughout the United States, have resulted in the fact that speakers of African American English typically live near other speakers of African American English (Labov, 2008; Massey & Denton, 1993; Massey & Lundy, 2001).

Surprisingly, relatively little linguistic and educational research has focused on African Americans who do *not* use features of African American English or who speak a more standardized variety of English, both of which might occur for several reasons, including where a person grew up, friends and networks, upbringing, education, and personal choice. Similarly, relatively little research has examined the speech of non–African Americans who use features of African American English in their speech. Because African American English is predominantly, but not exclusively, spoken by African Americans, the total number of people who use features of African American English may be greater than the number of people who identify as African American.

Many elements of African languages remain in contemporary African American English and in other varieties of English, including standardized English. Words such as *banana, banjo, gumbo, jamboree, mumbo jumbo, voodoo, yam,* and *zombie* have roots in African languages (Turner,

1949). Toepke and Serrano (1998) documented the migration of the lyrics and music of a Mende funeral song from Sierra Leone to the Sea Islands of South Carolina, where Gullah is spoken. This example is one illustration of the connections between African languages and African American English.

ATTITUDES TOWARD AFRICAN AMERICAN ENGLISH

Due to the history of racism and discrimination in the United States, the language patterns of African Americans have often been denigrated. African American English has been viewed as haphazard, substandard, undesirable, deviant, illogical, lazy, and broken. Yet there is no truth in such opinions about African American English or any other variety of English. Lippi-Green (1997) explained that negative and incorrect ideas about African American English are found throughout society, including in the media. In books, on TV, in films, and in music, the public receives mixed messages about a variety of English that is often admired as being cool but is also often looked down on as being unprofessional, sloppy, or incorrect.

Anyone can hold misperceptions about and negative attitudes toward African American English and its speakers, even African Americans themselves. For example, the film *Akeelah and the Bee* (Atchison, 2006) explored issues of education in the African American community. In one scene, Akeelah Anderson, an African American girl who attends a predominantly African American school in South Los Angeles, converses with Dr. Joshua Larabee, an African American professor of English. When Akeelah asks Dr. Larabee, "Ain't you got a job?", her use of the nonstandardized English phrase "Ain't you got" instead of the standardized English phrase "Don't you have" sparks his criticism.

> DR. LARABEE: Do me a favor. Leave the ghetto talk outside, all right?
>
> AKEELAH: Ghetto talk? I don't talk ghetto.
>
> DR. LARABEE: [in a mocking tone] "Ain't you got a job?" You use that language to fit in with your friends. Here, you will speak properly or you won't speak at all. Understood?

In this scene, Dr. Larabee mocks Akeelah's nonstandardized English. He assumes that Akeelah's language indicates that she comes from the ghetto and that she speaks the way she does because of peer group influence. Even more harshly, he orders her to change the way she speaks or to be silent.

A STUDENT'S PERSPECTIVE

"I have heard the argument made by an Appalachian English speaker that his acknowledged nonstandardized variety is acceptable because it is old and unchanging (i.e., a local standard), whereas African American English is unstable and based on slang, therefore deserving of no respect. It is interesting to me that some of the most vehement proponents against one English variety or another speak a very marked variety themselves."

Despite the many widespread and deeply held misperceptions about African American English (and many other varieties of English), the antidote to these stereotypes and inaccuracies is the willingness to hear and appreciate the variations that lend complexity and character to language. On a linguistic level, languages and language varieties are amazingly nuanced, unique, and innovative. On a social level, languages and language varieties are crucial vehicles for transmitting culture, history, personality, and identity.

THE VALUE OF AFRICAN AMERICAN LANGUAGE AND CULTURE

Language varieties hold inherent value as markers of culture and identity. As a result, some speakers of African American English, including students, may feel shame, insecurity, and embarrassment when they operate within a society that expects them to speak standardized English. Educators who teach African American English–speaking students have a special role to play in understanding these students' personal and cultural experiences and helping them navigate comfortably between African American English and standardized English.

A Dilemma for Students

When students come to school speaking African American English, they are aware that many of their relatives, friends, and neighbors speak similarly to themselves. They may also be aware that many of their educators do not speak African American English. The message that African American English–speaking students may internalize from this situation is that educators expect them to learn a new way of communicating, which may be at odds with their home language and culture. Smitherman (2000) described this "push-pull" that many African American students face in classrooms and schools. Carter (2007) further notes that as some African American students push harder to assimilate to mainstream academic culture in order to succeed in school, they may feel forced to pull away from their home communities. Most people would find it difficult to accept a message, even an indirect message, that they have to suppress part of their linguistic identity to operate within mainstream culture. African Americans, with their specific social and cultural history, often live this reality every day.

Many African American teachers also feel the tensions that Smitherman (2000) and Carter (2007) describe; indeed, Du Bois (1903) first described the "double consciousness" that many African Americans may feel when they navigate the social and professional demands of U.S. society. African American educators may find that they switch not only linguistically but also culturally between the language of their communities and the schools in which they teach. Other African American educators may find that they employ features of African American English in their classroom teaching to build rapport with their African American students (Foster, 1989).

Identity conflicts can also arise for educators and students in the form of dueling expectations. Many speakers of African American English feel compelled to shed their home linguistic patterns to succeed in a mainstream climate, yet they may also be highly invested in maintaining what they perceive to be their authentic African American speech and culture. In the film *Voices of North Carolina* (Hutcheson, 2005), such sentiments were expressed by Richard Brown, an African American from Durham, North Carolina.

> Particularly in the African American community, there is this idea that yes, you know, you can speak in a much more relaxed, intimate Black speech in certain spaces, and then in other spaces you have to speak a much more common English. And, for some people, there's an internal struggle about should you really do that. Should you really be trying to talk like White folk? Or should you always, all the time, no matter what setting you are in speak the same way—speak the way your mama taught you to speak?

Just as Smitherman (2000) and Carter (2007) discussed, Richard Brown also implicitly referred to the concept of "keeping it real" in African American culture. "Keeping it real" expresses the idea that even though the norms of White society may prevail in most social institutions, internal respect for African American culture, which includes respect for African American English, is essential.

Much research has investigated general attitudes surrounding African American English. Tucker and Lambert (1969) conducted the first systematic study of attitudes toward African American English, and their work has been replicated many times. They obtained evaluative judgments from 150 listeners and found that on a range of personal characteristics, listeners gave lower ratings to the voices of speakers of African American English and higher ratings to the voices of speakers of other varieties. In fact, listeners gave the lowest ratings to the African American speakers on the characteristics of *speech, education, talent,* and *intelligence,* indicating that the listeners' perceptions were most negative in these areas.

Fogel and Ehri (2000) also reviewed a number of studies that found that educators tend to rate African American English–speaking students as less intelligent, less confident, and less likely to succeed than students who speak in a more standardized way. Perceptions and beliefs often affect the feedback that educators give students. Therefore, biases against African American English may affect everyday interactions with students who speak this variety and may skew educators' academic expectations of them as well. Speaking and writing in African American English have even been factors in African American students' disproportional placement in remedial classes and in special education, both in the past and today (Cartledge & Dukes, 2008; Harry & Anderson, 1995; Keulen, Weddington, & DeBose, 1998).

Classroom work containing features of African American English and other varieties of English is often evaluated as inferior to otherwise equivalent work containing standardized English. Godley, Sweetland, Wheeler, Minnici, and Carpenter (2006) reported similar findings:

> Teachers are more likely to give lower evaluations to work presented orally by African American students, even when that work is equal in quality to work presented by White students. . . . Studies demonstrate that White teachers negatively evaluate the intelligence, social characteristics, and academic potential of children who speak in a recognizably African American style. (p. 31)

When students who speak nonstandardized varieties of English perceive that their language is devalued in school and that they are not receiving appropriate feedback from educators, they may feel discouraged from continuing their education. They may also perceive that their own culture, family, friends, and even they themselves are being devalued. In turn, they may lose confidence in school and in their educators. They may even resist the devaluation of their language and culture in academic settings by disengaging from the standardized English–speaking school culture and climate altogether.

Some African American English–speaking students might go in a different direction and accommodate as much as possible to the standardized English–speaking culture. Much educational literature has been devoted to understanding the concept that has come to be known as "sounding White" or "acting White," which refers to the academic bind felt by some African Americans who fear that any attempt to do well in school is seen by others as trying to act White (Fordham, 1996; Fordham & Ogbu, 1986; Ogbu, 2003). The idea of sounding and acting White as a way of achieving educational success is complex. African American students who use standardized English and resist using African American English may be stigmatized by other African Americans who see their linguistic choices as snubbing the local language variety and, as a result, their cultural background. At the same time, even if African American students sound and act in ways that are interpreted as being White, they may still not be accepted by White peers, whether due to prejudice or to a range of social factors.

Carter (2007) provided a comprehensive view concerning Fordham and Ogbu's claims that African American students may make sweeping rejections of White, middle-class culture in ways that hinder their educational success and social mobility. Carefully compiled evidence suggests that even though some African American students may sometimes reject White, middle-class styles of speech and behavior, most of them also understand that educational attainment leads to social mobility. Carter (2007) further emphasized the particular successes of African American students who are "multicultural navigators," individuals who adhere to the norms of the mainstream White society while still maintaining and respecting African American culture and history.

To help all students address issues of language, behavior, and racial identity in educational settings, Tatum (2003) encouraged educators to discuss the concept of culture with students. In her work, Tatum explored the racial understandings that students have, highlighted the role that development plays in racial identity, and provided guidelines to help in tough discussions both in and outside of the classroom.

A Dilemma for Educators

Beliefs about the use of African American English in educational settings lie along a wide continuum. Some educators may wonder how best to teach students who speak African American English to succeed in mainstream environments while still valuing their linguistic and cultural heritage. Others may believe it is altogether inappropriate for students to use features of African American English in school contexts. Students' use of African American English may be perceived as a mark of defiance or as a signal of rejection of school culture. Others may even feel that African American English is a substandard form of English that indicates a student's incapacity for linear thinking or logical analysis.

Numerous studies have reported these wide-ranging attitudes that educators have about African American English, documenting attitudes that are positive as well as negative (Godley et al., 2006; Goodman & Buck, 1973; Terry, 2008). Because educators may hold strong opinions about students' use of African American English, serious cultural and academic misunderstandings may arise between educators who speak standardized English and students who speak African American English, particularly when each person assumes that the other understands them and is understood by them. African American English–speaking students may even receive differential treatment in the classroom because of prejudice against this variety of English, lowered educational expectations for students who use this variety, and less tolerance for these students.

Tensions surrounding the use of African American English may also be a result of unfamiliarity with this language variety. Wilder (2000) reported that since around 1980, nearly 90% of the teaching force in the United States has been comprised of White teachers, while 30% of students are African American. Two-thirds of all African American teachers work in the South. Educators and students who come from different racial, ethnic, and cultural backgrounds may be unaware of, confused by, or ill equipped to understand each other's linguistic and cultural behaviors. Yet, whereas nonstandardized English–speaking students are made to learn the standardized language and culture, educators who are largely familiar with and teach the standardized language and culture are not, in most cases, made to do the reverse—to learn the linguistic and cultural patterns of their nonstandardized English–speaking students. These inequalities may cause cultural, social, and academic rifts and resentments, as well as unintentional misunderstandings, as educators and students alike may assume that the other is "operating according to identical speech and cultural conventions" when, in fact, different norms may be in use (Kochman, 1981, p. 8).

Educators may advocate that their students use standardized English because they know that speaking and writing according to accepted standards have many tangible, real-world benefits. Educators know that students who are comfortable with using standardized English are not only more likely to be told that they sound educated; they are also probably more likely to get ahead in their educational and professional pursuits and are less likely to face discrimination based on the sound of their voices (Baugh, 2000; Bullock, 2006; Massey & Lundy, 2001). In one experiment, six African American applicants were sent to interview for secretarial positions at 100 sites. Those applicants who spoke in standardized English rather than African American English were given longer interviews and were more likely to be offered a job (Terrell & Terrell, 1983).

At the same time, simply using standardized English does not *guarantee* that an African American student will be able to succeed in school and in life. In a society where many opportunities hinge on a person's race, perceptions that a speaker of African American English is attempting to sound White may have positive effects, negative effects, or no effect at all on that individual's educational and occupational success. African Americans who speak standardized English still might be passed over for a job simply because they are African American, as has been documented by Bertrand and Mullainathan (2003). In their study, the researchers responded to help-wanted ads in Boston and Chicago newspapers with fictitious résumés, half of which had very African American–sounding names and half of which had very White–sounding names. Those with White names received 50% more callbacks for interviews. Other studies have documented inequalities in wages that result from sounding African American. Grogger (2008) found that African American workers whose speech is distinctly identified as "sounding Black" earn salaries that are 10% lower than White workers with comparable skills. He also found that Whites who "sound Black" earn 6% lower salaries than other Whites. In addition, he found that even African American workers whose speech was *not* distinctly identified as "sounding Black" earned 2% less than comparably skilled White workers. As these studies make clear, racial discrimination persists in the labor market.

The goals of wanting to honor African American English–speaking students' cultural and linguistic heritage while also preparing them to live and work in a standardized English–speaking society are thus complicated for educators and students. In other communities, including immigrant communities, students similarly face pressure to assimilate to English in order to do well in school and in life. While there are many school and community programs in place to aid students who grow up speaking a foreign language in their quest to learn English, there are few programs in place to help speakers of nonstandardized varieties of English, including African American English. The general sentiment is that native English speakers should be able to produce standardized English forms no matter what their background. As Baldwin (1985) contended, however, succeeding at school should not require African American students to abandon their linguistic and cultural heritage. He stated, "A child cannot be taught by anyone whose demand, essentially, is that the child repudiate his experience, and all that gives him sustenance, and enter a limbo in which he will no longer be black, and in which he knows that he can never become white" (p. 652). It is therefore important to understand the language patterns that students bring with them into the classroom to best help all students attain academic success.

FEATURES OF AFRICAN AMERICAN ENGLISH

Speakers of African American English tend to share a group of linguistic features. Some features overlap with those of other varieties of English, including Southern English (as discussed in Chapter 3), but many features are unique to African American English. These features may also vary in the language patterns of individuals.

Sound

The question of whether a person sounds African American often has to do with the ways that sounds function within and across languages. Some sound-related features of African American English are shared by other varieties of American English, especially Southern English, while other sound-related features are unique to African American English. Sound-related features of African American English often have important educational implications for students who use these variants.

The pronunciation of *ask*. Listeners often notice that many African American English speakers pronounce the word *ask* the same as the word *axe*. Not only do people tend to notice this pronunciation, but it is also often stigmatized and even mocked. Yet the production of *ask* as *axe* has existed in the English language for 1,000 years. For example, Chaucer's *The Canterbury Tales*, written in 1386, contains the following line in the Prologue to the Wife of Bath's Tale, "But that I axe why that the fifthe man was noon housbonde to the Samaritan" (Chaucer, 2005, p. 211). When translated, this line reads, "All I ask is, why wasn't the fifth man/ The lawful spouse of the Samaritan?" (Chaucer, 2008, p. 219). In Old English, the verb *ascian* (meaning "to ask") underwent a sound change in which two pronunciations were widely used at the same time. Speakers in the north of England pronounced *ascian* as "askian," while speakers in the Midlands and the south of England pronounced it as "axeian." This reversal of two neighboring sounds or syllables is called *metathesis*, which occurs often in words that have complex sound blends. As Coates (2009) reports, for example, the old English pronunciation of the word *third* is "thred," which comes from the word *three*. More contemporary examples of metathesis include the words *jewelry*, which is often pronounced as "jew-luh-ree" instead of "jew-el-ree," *nuclear*, which is often pronounced as "nuke-you-lur" instead of "new-klee-ur," and *chipotle*, which is often pronounced as "chih-pole-tay" instead of "chih-pote-lay."

While the pronunciation of *ask* as *axe* is considered to be a nonstandardized pronunciation today, it is nevertheless very common. Many African Americans pronounce *ask* as *axe*, as do many speakers in the South, in Appalachia, in other pockets of the United States, in the Caribbean, and in parts of the United Kingdom. Part of the reason that this pronunciation is almost instantly noticed when it is used by African Americans is because it has come to be viewed as a stereotyped feature of African American English.

The *r* sound. In many varieties of English, the *r* sound may be absent or nearly absent. For example, if the *r* sound is absent, the word *father* is pronounced as "fahthah," and the word *hurt* is pronounced as "hut." The absence of *r* has been a feature of many regional American varieties, as well as British and Australian English; *r* sounds may be also absent in the pronunciations of speakers from New York, Boston, and Charleston.

The *r* sound may be absent in African American English, and specific linguistic patterns govern when this process occurs. In African American English, the *r* sound may be absent if it follows a vowel sound, as it does in the words *car, father, card, bigger, cardboard, court, beer, mother*, and *four*. The *r* sound is generally *not* absent when it follows a consonant sound, as in the words *approach, bring, principal, spring, okra*, and *April*. The *r* sound is also never absent when it begins a word, as in *red, reading*, and *run*, or when it begins a syllable, as in *garage*. This linguistic explanation applies to other varieties of English that have *r* absence as well.

The *th* sound. In standardized English, there are two ways that *th* is pronounced: a voiceless (or "soft") *th* sound, as in the words *think* and *thanks*, and a voiced (or "hard") *th* sound, as in the words *there* and *that*. In African American English, these *th* sounds can be pronounced either similarly to *or* differently from the ways *th* sounds are produced in standardized English, depending on where the sound is located in the word.

Specific linguistic patterns govern the pronunciation of the voiced *th* sound, as found in the words *this, these, those, that, they, smooth, neither*, and *either*. In African American English, when the voiced *th* sound occurs at the beginning of a word, it can be pronounced as a *d* sound. The word *that* might thus be pronounced as "dat," *these* might be pronounced as "dese," *those* might be pronounced as "doze," and *they* might be pronounced as "day." When the voiced *th* sound occurs in the middle or at the end of a word, it can be pronounced as a *d* sound or a *v* sound. The word *smooth* might thus be pronounced as "smoov," and *neither* might be pronounced as "needer" or as "neever."

Linguistic patterns also govern the pronunciation of the voiceless *th* sound, found in words such as *think, thanks, thin, thistle, both, earth, myth,* and *with*. In African American English, when the voiceless *th* sound occurs at the beginning of a word, it is usually pronounced just as it is in standardized English. (Sometimes African American English speakers with African and Caribbean heritage might pronounce a word-initial voiceless *th* sound like a *t*, so that the word *think* might be pronounced as "tink" and *thanks* might be pronounced as "tanks.")

When the voiceless *th* sound occurs in the middle or at the end of a word, speakers of African American English can pronounce the sound in three ways: as a *t* sound, as an *f* sound, or as a glottal stop sound (i.e., the sound that happens when the voice stops in the middle of the word *uh-oh*). For example, in African American English, the word *with* can be pronounced as "wif," as "wit," or as "wi'."

These alternative pronunciations of the voiced and voiceless *th* sounds are never random, but rather occur in line with phonetic rules that are based on whether the *th* sound is voiced or voiceless and where the *th* sound occurs in the context of a word. These variants of the *th* sound in African American English are directly linked to the sound patterns found in Gullah and languages of West Africa, which tend not to have the voiced or voiceless *th* sounds in their sound inventories (Turner, 1949).

Final consonants. In standardized English, the *b, d,* and *g* sounds are voiced sounds (in contrast to their voiceless counterpart sounds, *p, t,* and *k*). In comparison, in African American English, the *b, d,* and *g* sounds can be devoiced (that is, rendered as the *p, t,* or *k* sounds, respectively) when they occur at the end of a word or syllable. For example, *lad* may be pronounced as "lat," *lag* may be pronounced as "lack," and *lab* may be pronounced as "lap." Sometimes the final consonant may sound similar to a glottal stop sound. Thus, a speaker of African American English may pronounce the word *badlands* either as "batlands" (the *d* sound has been devoiced and rendered as the *t* sound) or as "ba'lands" (the *d* sound has been devoiced and rendered as a glottal stop). In African American English, final consonant sounds may also be absent altogether, so that the words *five* and *fine* may both be pronounced similarly to the word *fie*.

The nasal consonant sounds *m* and *n* may also vary in African American English, as they may be pronounced as nasal vowels rather than as nasal consonants. Standardized English does not have nasal vowels (although other languages, like Brazilian Portuguese and French, do). As a result, it is difficult to represent these unique sounds from African American English with the spelling conventions of standardized English. In African American English, the word *ran* might sound similar to "reh" and the words *man* and *ma'am* might sound similar to "meh." In these words, the final *n* and *m* sounds are almost absent, except for the fact that the *eh* sound has a nasal quality to it, much as the vowels in the French words *bon* and *vingt* do. Often, in African American English, nasalized *eh* vowel sounds have a longer duration than in standardized English.

Consonant blends. One major difference between African American English and standardized English concerns the reduction of clusters of consonants, such as *sk, nd, ts, kt, sts,* and *sks*. For almost any speaker of English, the reduction of consonant clusters happens frequently. Words such as *tactful* and *lists*, which contain complex consonant blends, are pronounced by most speakers of English as "tackful" and "liss." Similarly, most English speakers would pronounce a sentence such as "She gave her *best* guess" as "She gave her bess guess."

In African American English, this same sound-related process of reducing consonant clusters to a single consonant sound occurs as well, only much more frequently and in a wider range of linguistic contexts than in standardized English. For example, African American English speakers may pronounce *test* as "tes," *desk* as "des," *walked* as "walk," *find* as "fine," *hand* as "han," and a phrase such as *west end* as "wes end." Subtle and complex linguistic rules govern the higher frequency and wider range of conditions under which African American English speakers may reduce consonant clusters, just as nuanced linguistic rules govern the conditions and frequency of consonant cluster reduction in standardized English.

In addition to reducing consonant clusters more frequently than speakers of standardized English do, African American English speakers may vary in their pronunciation of certain consonants within clusters. Sometimes in African American English and in other varieties of English, the *r* sound that occurs within consonant clusters may be reduced. Thus, in a word such as *professor*, the *pr* cluster may be pronounced as it is in standardized English, or it may be reduced, such that the word sounds more like "puhfessor." In another example, the word *throw* might be pronounced similarly to *though*. In addition, in African American English the process can occur in reverse—*r* sounds may sometimes be inserted into words, creating new consonant blends, as in pronunciations such as "fruneral" for *funeral* and "brootiful" for *beautiful.* This sound-related process occurs in other varieties of English as well, as in the common pronunciation "sherbert" for *sherbet.*

African American English also features other unique consonant blends. In African American English, *str* clusters may sometimes be pronounced as *scr,* such that the word *stream* may be pronounced as "scream," *street* as "skreet," *straight* as "skraight," *stretch* as "skretch," *strong* as "scrong," *destroy* as "deskroy," and *strawberry* as "scrawberry." This feature is also found in the Gullah language. Dandy (1991) pointed out that students' pronunciation of *str* clusters as *scr* is often stigmatized by those who do not recognize it as a patterned language feature. In Dandy's study, many of the African American students who used this feature were referred to speech pathologists.

The *ai* and *oy* sounds. Most speakers of African American English have a vowel merger in which the *ai* sound is pronounced similarly to the *ah* sound. This process is also found in Southern English, as we reported in Chapter 3. Thus, the word *time* may be pronounced as "tom," *bye* may be pronounced as "bah," and *mile* may be pronounced as "mall." In addition, in African American English, as in Southern English, there is variation in the *oy* sound. For this feature, *oil* may be pronounced as "oll" or "all," *boil* may be pronounced as "boll" or "ball," and *toil* may be pronounced as "toll" or "tall."

Vowel mergers. Speakers of African American English may also pronounce words that contain *i* and *e* before nasal consonants (*n, m,* and *ng* sounds) in nearly the same ways. The word *pen* may be pronounced as "pin," *ten* as "tin," and *hem* as "him." In addition, words such as *feel* may be pronounced as "fill," and *fill* may be pronounced as "feel." *Heel* may be pronounced as "hill," and *hill* may be pronounced as "heel." Words such as *fail* may be pronounced as "fell," *hail* may be pronounced as "hell," and *bail* may be pronounced as "bell." These sound patterns are similar to those of Southern English discussed in Chapter 3.

The *oo* sound. A unique feature of African American English is that the vowel sound *yu* may sound similar to *oo* following a consonant. Words such as *Houston* may sound similar to "Hooston," *interview* may sound similar to "intervoo," *review* may sound similar to "revoo," and *computer* may sound similar to "compooter."

The *air* sound. Another feature that is fairly unique to African American English is that the *air* sound at the end of a word may sound similar to *ur*. For example, the word *hair* may sound similar to "her," *care* may sound similar to "cur," and *there* may sound similar to "thur." Phrases such as *carry out* may sound similar to "curry out," and the name of the state *Maryland* may sound similar to "Murrland." The media have played a role in popularizing this feature of African American English. Songs by hip-hop artists such as Chingy, J-Kwon, and Nelly, who are from St. Louis, Missouri, have featured words with this variant of *r* in their music since 2001 (Blake, Fix, & Shousterman, 2009). In the song "Hot in Herre," Nelly (2002) not only pronounces the word *here* as "her" in his lyrics but also uses nonstandardized spelling to represent the variation ("herre") in his song's title.

Educational implications. The fact that African American English–speaking students may differ in their pronunciations of certain consonant and vowel sounds can result in serious educational effects, consequences, and implications. Students who speak African American English may have the same inventory of sounds in their speech as other students do, but due to differences found in African American English, students' written and spoken language may manifest somewhat different patterns than those manifested by other students. To communicate respect for both African American English and standardized English while still helping students achieve success in mainstream educational environments, it is important to avoid statements such as "Don't leave off your endings of words" and "Don't drop your *r*'s," which may be perceived by students as rebukes. Instead, students should be made aware of variation in English through such questions as "In standardized English, what is the pattern for how an *r* is pronounced?" Referring to "different" rather than "correct" versus "incorrect" pronunciations also removes negative value judgments from the discussions of linguistic variants.

Studies of the processes through which students learn how to associate specific sounds with specific letters reveal how differences in pronunciation patterns may affect how African American English–speaking students spell and read. When they first come to school, many children are familiar with names, including their own and those of their family members and friends, and they may also be familiar with labels and brand names for such items as clothing and toys. Craig and Washington (2004) noted, however, that names and labels often violate conventional spelling rules, particularly those names and labels that are developed in African American English, because the sound patterns of this variety are not codified in the written system of standardized English. For example, African American children may come to school knowing how to spell and pronounce the name *Kwame* (pronounced "KWAHM-ee"). By analogy, they may mispronounce names that may be unfamiliar to them, such as Blake, which is spelled similarly to Kwame but is not pronounced "BLAH-key." In comparison, children who are familiar with the name Blake but who are not familiar with the sound–spelling relationships found in African American English may, by analogy to names such as Blake, mispronounce the similarly spelled name Kwame as having just one syllable, "Kwaim."

Craig and Washington (2004) further noted that when African American English–speaking students work to apply their decoding skills for reading familiar items, such as names, to reading unfamiliar items, they may encounter greater challenges as a result of the differences between the sound and spelling patterns of African American English and those of standardized English. For example, an African American child who is used to pronouncing and spelling the name *Kwame* may encounter difficulty when learning to decode words such as *blame, dame,* and *fame.* As Labov (2006, p. 5) explained, "the most important challenge for the struggling reader who wants to master the vowels of the English alphabet is the silent *-e* rule," which operates in words like *blame.* Moreover, students who come to school speaking a nonstandardized variety of English may face additional difficulties when they are taught that some spellings of words have silent *e,* yet they know that in similarly spelled words that occur in their home variety, the *e* is pronounced.

The abstract sound–letter correspondences of English may be difficult for many students to learn. Labov (2006) noted that while many useful rules for working out the relations of sound and spelling in English exist, these rules also have many exceptions and complications

> due to changes in the language that took place after the [English] spelling system was established. . . . [E]ven for good readers, it takes about two years longer to learn to read English than languages like Spanish or Hungarian with a simpler system. (p. 2)

For African American English speakers who are learning to read, relating the alphabet to speech patterns may be more difficult, since the sound and grammar patterns that the students have grown up with differ in several key ways from those of standardized English.

Labov (1972, 2006) and Labov and Baker (2003) conducted extensive studies of how variations in African American English–speaking students' vowel and consonant sounds impact their educational experiences and their educational success, especially when it comes to learning sound–letter correspondence. Consider the word *their.* Spelling this word might be confusing for African American English–speaking students who pronounce the *th* sound as a *d* sound, because they may wonder why the first sound of the word that they pronounce as "deir" is not spelled with a *d,* as it sounds to them, but rather with a *th*. African American English–speaking students who pronounce *birthday* and *with* as "birfday" and "wif" may similarly wonder why these words are spelled with *th*, not *f*. For these reasons, it may be more challenging for students who speak African American English to learn sound–letter correspondences, and these challenges may directly affect the speed and fluency with which they learn to read.

In another example, to African American English–speaking students who pronounce the word *hand* as "han," it may seem particularly confusing why the letter *d* needs to be included in the spelling of the word. Gilyard (1996) described how words that are homophones in African American English account for many misspellings that he sees in his students' compositions. He gives the example of one student who, due to consonant cluster reduction, spelled *mind* as *mine* in the sentence, "I really wouldn't mine having an Acura Legend" (p. 69). Likewise, if an African American English–speaking student pronounces *cold* similarly to *code*, the fact that the letter *l* has no corresponding sound in the student's spoken version of the word may lead the student to omit the *l* when writing the word. Similarly, because African American English–speaking students may pronounce *told* as "toll," *find* as "fine," *mist* as "miss," and *passed* as "pass," they may face challenges in determining how to spell these words.

Variations in the sounds of African American English may also affect how African American English–speaking students create rhymes. Often, rhyming is a skill that is drilled in schools as part of learning phonics, but African American English–speaking students may come to school with knowledge of different rhyme patterns because of linguistic differences. African American English–speaking students may rhyme words such as *door* and *dough*, due to *r* absence; *turf* and *earth*, due to variation in pronouncing the voiceless *th* sound as the *f* sound; and *kind* and *fine*, due to consonant cluster reduction. Serpell, Baker, and Sonnenschein (2005) also found that African American children tended to have less exposure to and be less familiar than White children with traditional European-based nursery rhymes, which affected their sensitivity to standardized English rhyme patterns. The greater familiarity that White students have with standardized English rhyme patterns gives White students an advantage in educational situations, in which they may be asked to produce traditional or expected rhymes within the conventions of standardized English, which they already know.

STRATEGIES FOR EDUCATORS

To promote the development of sensitivity to rhyme patterns, educators can help younger students practice various types of nursery rhymes, jump-rope rhymes, and hand-clapping games. We encourage providing students with the opportunity to rhyme in both standardized English and African American English. Educators may lead a discussion of the differences in rhyming schemes that the students hear and use, thereby increasing all students' sensitivity to sound patterns and linguistic awareness.

For older students, educators may address aspects of standardized English rhyme sensitivity by integrating word games and other aspects of verbal play into classroom instruction. Students may play rhyming word games or they may generate tongue twisters, riddles, jokes, and puns, in standardized English as well as in African American English, noting and comparing differences.

Students may also explore rhyming techniques through exercises in which they compose and analyze their own poems or song lyrics. Students can be encouraged to discuss how words that rhyme in African American English may be similar to or different from rhyme patterns found in standardized English. Exercises in which students compose their own songs and poetry help enhance students' knowledge of and sensitivity to rhyme, syllables, and the conventions of word formation (Goodman, 2003). In addition, by providing all students with situations in which they are encouraged to practice expressing themselves in their home varieties as well as in standardized English, students will develop their linguistic versatility.

Educators can also plan activities that allow students to compare and contrast poems written in different language varieties, including African American English. For example, Paul Laurence Dunbar was an African American poet who, as the only African American in his high school, became acutely aware of language differences in his Ohio community. As a result, in his own poetry, he sought to show the beauty of both African American English and the style of poetry of the European tradition. Dunbar's poems that use standardized American English (for example, the poem "Sympathy") and those that use African American English (such as the poem "Little Brown Baby") are excellent for illustrating and teaching the linguistic differences between these varieties (see Paul Laurence Dunbar homepage, 2003). Students may read Dunbar's poems and consider such questions as: How would a poem written in African American English be different if it were written in standardized English, and vice versa? What are the advantages and disadvantages of each style? Students can also compose their own poetry in the style of poets such as Dunbar, using features of standardized English as well as African American English.

Sound-related differences in speech production, especially those related to consonant cluster reduction, can also affect grammar. As mentioned earlier, speakers of African American English may frequently reduce the sounds in consonant blends, producing them instead with only one consonant sound. For example, the *st* blend in *test*, the *sk* blend in *desk*, and the *kt* blend in *walked* and *talked* may be pronounced as "tes," "des," "walk," and "talk." In words such as *walked* and *talked*, when the *kt* sound in *walked* is pronounced as a *k* sound, African American English speakers may sound as though they are not marking the past tense (for example, they may pronounce "I walked" and "I walk" the same). An African American English speaker who pronounces *walked* like *walk* may write "walk" for *walked* as well. Especially in writing, spelling the word *walked* as "walk" in a past tense sentence (e.g., "I walk to school yesterday" instead of "I walked to school yesterday") may be perceived as being a serious standardized English error in subject–verb agreement, even though the spelling form is rooted in the linguistic fact that speakers of African American English tend to reduce consonant clusters more frequently than do speakers of standardized English.

In a study conducted by Labov and Baker (2003), an African American third-grader who was asked to read out loud the sentence "I played it cool and took a sip of my Coke" pronounced the verb *played* as "play." Because the second verb, *took*, was pronounced in the past tense, as it was written, it was clear that the student understood the sentence was in the past tense. Most likely, Labov and Baker determined, the student's pronunciation of *played* as "play" was due to use of consonant cluster reduction, not to any misunderstanding as to whether the sentence was in the past tense. Educators may wish to explain to African American English–speaking students that their linguistic patterns allow them to reduce consonant blends, meaning that they may need to pay particular attention to pronouncing the past tense endings of verbs aloud in situations that call for the use of standardized English.

Sometimes, African American English–speaking students who recognize that there are issues with how they mark the past tense in their speech and writing may attempt to emphasize the fact that they are communicating in the past tense by doubly pronouncing the endings on past tense words—particularly in cases in which the past tense cannot be understood by context clues. For example, in sentences without other apparent time markers, African American English speakers may emphasize that they are speaking in the past tense by pronouncing *walked* as "walkded" and *talked* as "talkded." Similarly, African American English–speaking students may emphasize that a given noun is plural by pronouncing the word in a way that separates the plural marker from the consonant cluster. Thus, a student may pronounce a word such as *desks* as "deskes" or, if the consonant cluster has been reduced, as "desses." Students may even write these hypercorrected forms, which tend to be perceived as serious grammatical and spelling errors in standardized English. Other students may not mark the *-s* on plural nouns, which is a feature that is revisited in the grammar section.

Because sound-related language differences may pose particular challenges for African American English–speaking students who are learning to read, such students may have continued difficulty with reading and writing in standardized English, which may, in turn, negatively impact their scores on academic and psychometric assessments. For all these reasons, African American English–speaking students who face linguistic difficulties with learning standardized English may lose confidence in the alphabet and may doubt their ability to read. They may also give little credit to decoding strategies such as "Just sound it out" or "Just write it like it sounds," since such strategies may contradict the students' understanding of how sounds work. Faced with these confusing situations, some African American English–speaking students may doubt the importance and the validity of educational assessments and lose faith in the educational system altogether.

Educators of African American English–speaking students may also lose confidence. They may doubt the ability of African American English–speaking students to learn or question their own ability to teach concepts that are central to phonics, rhyming, and reading to their African American English speakers. Instructions such as "Let's sound the word out" to students whose repertoire of sounds differs from that of standardized English might not work well for the educator or for the student. Instead, helping African American English–speaking students understand how the sound system of standardized English is similar to and different from that of African American English is crucial knowledge as these students make their way through the educational system.

Grammar

Grammatical features of African American English may be more noticeable and distinct than its sound-related features. A speaker of African American English may be able to use some nonstandardized sound features without their being noticed, but nonstandardized grammatical features tend to be noticed and are more often highly stigmatized by the general public. It is important to remember, however, that regardless of the public's greater stigmatization of the grammatical features of African American English, these features are nonetheless just as systematic and regular as sound-related features are, and they are just as systematic and regular as the grammatical features of standardized English.

Ain't. The word *ain't* is commonly used as a helping or linking verb in African American English (as well as Southern English). In sentences such as "I ain't seen her" and "He ain't shy," the word *ain't* can replace the verbs *haven't, hasn't, isn't,* and *aren't.* In African American English, *ain't* may also be used where other speakers use *didn't,* as in "I ain't do my homework last night" for "I didn't do my homework last night" and "I ain't go nowhere!" for "I didn't go anywhere!"

Educators can help students compare and contrast the use of *ain't* in African American English with the ways that other verb forms are used in standardized English. When differences in patterns of African American English and patterns of standardized English are presented in ways that value both varieties, students will be better able to recognize their own ways of speaking and writing and develop their facility with standardized English.

STRATEGIES FOR EDUCATORS

The book *Don't Say Ain't* (Smalls, 2004) is an excellent tool for discussing *ain't* with young students. The book is set in the 1950s and the protagonist, Diana, works to straddle two worlds, that of her Harlem neighborhood and that of the magnet school she is selected to attend. When her new magnet school teacher tells her not to use *ain't* in the classroom, Diana longs for the language of her friends and community, but then she learns that her teacher uses *ain't* as well, albeit outside the classroom.

Students can learn more about the use of *ain't* versus *isn't, hasn't,* or *didn't* by examining passages written in African American English that contain *ain't* and comparing them to how those passages would be written in standardized English. For example, Lorraine Hansberry's play *A Raisin in the Sun* (1959, p. 9) includes the following dialogue:

"Walter Lee Younger . . . it is time for you to get up! Ain't he out yet?"

"Out? He ain't hardly got in there good yet."

Students may circle each instance of *ain't* in the dialogue and rewrite the dialogue into standardized English, practicing replacing *ain't* with *isn't, hasn't,* or *didn't.*

To further reinforce similarities and differences in the language patterns of African American English and standardized

English, educators and students may also work with excerpts from texts written in standardized English and consider what rules govern the use of *isn't, hasn't* and *didn't*. Discussions about the use of *ain't* and *isn't* in standardized English compared to African American English raise students' linguistic awareness and prompt them to consider these issues when composing their own work.

These exercises have been designed to help students uncover and practice the rules of standardized English by examining texts, rather than using grammar drills and timed writings. As noted by the National Council of Teachers of English, it is best to avoid using decontextualized and often monotonous grammar exercises (Stover & NCTE Standing Committee on Teacher Preparation and Certification, 2006). Instead, exercises can be designed in ways that help students focus on particular language features as they are used in various specific texts.

Multiple negatives. Many varieties of English, including African American English, allow for the use of multiple negatives within one sentence or clause. For example, Labov (1972) recalls an African American teenager named Speedy, who was discussing pigeon coops in a conversation with some of his friends. Speedy, chuckling, uttered the sentence, "It ain't no cat can't get in no coop." Speedy was denying that cats are a problem, arguing that there isn't any cat around that can get into any pigeon coop.

Speakers of African American English commonly use multiple negation to add emphasis to statements, which is an important point for educators to remember. Gumperz and Hernández-Chavez (1972, p. 102) described a situation in which a student read a passage from an autobiographical essay to his teacher. When the student got to the sentence, "This lady didn't have no sense," the teacher stopped him and asked, "What would be a standard English alternate for this sentence?" The student replied, "She didn't have any sense. But not this lady: *she didn't have no sense*." As this anecdote makes clear, speakers of African American English may use multiple negatives to impart special emphatic meaning to their speech and writing.

Helping or linking forms of *be*. A grammatical feature that is often noticed and marked as an error in African American English–speaking students' writing is variation in the helping or linking forms of the verb *to be*. Speakers of African American English have three choices for how to use these forms: The verb forms may be fully produced, they may be contracted, or they may be absent. In comparison, speakers of standardized English have only two choices: These forms may be fully produced, or they may be contracted. As an example, standardized English speakers might say "He is funny" (a full form) or "He's funny" (a contracted form). African American English speakers may use either of these forms, but they also have the option of saying "He funny" (with the *is* form absent). In another example, standardized English speakers might say "We are running to the store" or "We're running to the store." In addition to these choices, speakers of African American English may say "We running to the store," with the *are* form absent.

In African American English, the helping and linking forms of *to be* can only be absent when the subject of the sentence is *you, he, she, it, we,* or *they*—never when the subject is *I*. The same rules apply for contraction in standardized English and in African American English. For example, African American English speakers may say "you running," "he running," "she running," and "they running," but not "I running." In addition, the helping and linking *to be* verb in African American English generally may not be absent in the past tense. For example, African American English speakers may say "He thinking about me right now" and "He thinking about me today" but not "He thinking about me yesterday."

Rickford (1999) found that Creole languages spoken in Barbados, Guyana, Jamaica, Trinidad, and the South Carolina Sea Islands (where Gullah is spoken) also have absence of the helping and linking forms of *to be* to similar degrees and in similar linguistic contexts as in African American English. This comparative linguistic evidence is a reminder that the absence of helping or linking forms of *to be* in African American English does not indicate haphazard mistakes or linguistic deficiencies on the part of African American English speakers. Instead, variation in African American English reflects its linguistic heritage and points toward its connections with African languages and African-based Creoles.

Habitual or invariant forms of *be*. A frequently noticed and frequently parodied grammatical feature of African American English is the use of invariant *be*. Standardized English has no way of distinguishing habituality for the verb *to be*. Instead, speakers of standardized English mark habituality by using the present tense of *is* or *are* plus an adverb, such as *usually, typically, often,* or *regularly*. For example, a speaker of standardized English might say "The students typically miss class when the bus comes late" to indicate the habituality of the situation.

In comparison, African American English uses invariant *be* to convey habituality in a way that does not require the addition of words such as *usually* and *typically*. For example, a speaker of African American English might say "The students be missing class when the bus comes late" to indicate the habitual nature of the event. For these reasons, this use of *be* in African American English is often known as *habitual be*. In contrast, speakers of African American English would generally *not* say "The bus be late right now." Such a sentence would not make sense, because the habituality that is marked by the use of invariant *be* would contradict the sense of immediacy that the phrase "right now" entails. It is important to remember that the use of invariant *be* in African American English is regular, patterned, and predictable. When invariant *be* surfaces in African American English–speaking students' speech or writing, the aspect that is conveyed by the form is generally a habitual one.

Stressed *been*. A feature of African American English that is rarely, if ever, used by speakers of other varieties is stressed *BEEN* (pronounced "bin"; the form is capitalized to indicate emphasis). This use of *been*, which is stressed in pronunciation and paired with a main verb in the simple past tense, indicates that an event has happened in the *remote* past, a long time prior to the present time. Thus, an African American English–speaking student might state "I been finished my homework," meaning that the student finished it a long time ago, perhaps also implying that the listener should already know this information. An African American English–speaking student might also use this feature in a sentence such as "My teacher been gave us the test," indicating that the test was given a long time ago, or "I been learned the answer," indicating that the information was acquired in the remote past. If the feature is not understood, a crucial transfer of information and meaning may be lost (for more, see Green, 2002).

In another example, consider this statement in African American English: "I been married." A standardized English speaker might hear this sentence and perceive that the speaker means "I was married at one time, although I'm not married anymore." In African American English, however, the sentence "I been married" means "I have been married for a long time now, and I am still married." These differences in meaning may cause comprehension difficulties between speakers of standardized English and speakers of African American English if they do not understand each other's patterns of communication.

The *call -self* construction. A grammatical feature that involves the verb *to call* plus a personal reflexive pronoun is also frequently used in African American English but rarely, if ever, used by speakers of other varieties. In African American English, this feature describes a situation in which, in the opinion of the speaker (and others), someone has made an attempt to do something that is not meeting typical standards. If an African American English speaker says, for example, "He calls himself cooking," the speaker is producing the equivalent of "He thinks he's cooking, but he's merely playing around in the kitchen" (Green, 2002, p. 21).

Absence of -s inflections. There are three forms of *-s* used in standardized English that may be absent in African American English. First, *-s* is often absent in third-person singular verb forms. For example, an African American English speaker may say "He talk too much" for "He talks too much" or "She like cats" for "She likes cats." Second, final *-s* may be absent in possessive constructions, where standardized English would call for *-s*. For example, an African American English speaker may say "I'm going to my mama house" for "I'm going to my mama's house" or "Look at John hat" for "Look at John's hat." Third, *-s* in plural constructions may be absent. For example, speakers of African American English might say "Give me 50 cent" for "Give me 50 cents" or "Those dog should go home" for "Those dogs should go home."

STRATEGIES FOR EDUCATORS

In presentations that Anne has given, she asked educators the following questions: How many times have you taken off points for students who leave off *-s* on third-person singular verb forms or on plural nouns? How many points do you think such students lose over the course of their academic career? Is it possible that students could lose enough points on the basis of these linguistic differences that they would make bad grades in school and on standardized tests?

We encourage the reexamination of grading policies in light of information about language variation in African American English. When a missing *-s* surfaces in students' writing in situations that call for adherence to the conventions of standardized English, educators can explain to students the patterns underlying the absence of the *-s* and discuss with them how *-s* is used in standardized English. Students may not learn these patterns immediately, and they may need to be reminded of these conventions over time. Grading policies may also be revised to ensure that terms like "appropriate spelling" are clearly defined and to make sure that students understand what it means to have "subject–verb agreement."

Existential *it*. In African American English, *it is* or *it's* may be used to denote the existence of something in a way that is generally equivalent to the use of *there is, there's,* and *there are* in standardized English. For example, a speaker of African American English may say "It's some cake in the pantry," whereas in the same situation, a speaker of standardized English may say "There's some cake in the pantry." Similarly, a speaker of African American English may say "It's a pencil in the drawer" for the standardized English sentence "There's a pencil in the drawer." This feature may appear in African American English–speaking students' speech and writing.

Educational implications. For African American English–speaking students, learning to speak and write using the grammar conventions of standardized English can be a complicated process. One major issue, as we have noted, surrounds how the grammatical system of African American English interacts with its sound system in ways that differ from how sound and grammar interact in standardized English. For example, an African American English–speaking student who, due to consonant cluster reduction, pronounces words such as *joined* as "join" or *marked* as "mark" may, in turn, write "join" for *joined* and "mark" for *marked.* As a result, this student may face additional challenges with the recognition and production of grammatical particles (including the *-ed* that marks the past tense) in standardized English. On written homework that such students produce and on standardized tests, the use of words such as *mark* for *marked* and other sound-related grammatical variants may be viewed as evidence of a major grammatical error in standardized English. It is critical not to inadvertently overpenalize students whose language variants differ from those of standardized English.

Past tense forms in standardized English that are spelled and/or sound exactly like present tense forms may be particularly difficult for African American English speakers. Labov (1972) found that students who spoke African American English were able to correctly pronounce the past tense form of *read* in the sentence "Last month I read the sign," in which the phrase "last month" indicates the past tense. The sentence "When I passed by, I read the sign" posed much more difficulty. In this sentence, the African American English–speaking students tended to pronounce the verb *passed* as "pass," and they subsequently pronounced the verb *read* in its present tense form (they pronounced it as "reed," not "red"). These pronunciation differences indicated that the African American English–speaking students comprehended the sentences as being in the *present* tense, not the *past;* they interpreted the sentence as "When I pass by, I read the sign." It is therefore important to pay particular attention to helping students learn the different pronunciations that accompany past and present tense verb forms in standardized English.

Other sound differences in African American English have similar grammatical implications. African American English speakers may have absent or reduced final consonants, which may mean that contracted future tense forms may be difficult to recognize. For example, "You'll go there" may sound similar to "You go there," due to the absence of the final *l* sound in *you'll*. Similarly, *I'll* can be difficult to distinguish from *I*, both for African American English speakers who are decoding standardized English and for speakers of a standardized variety of English who are decoding written or spoken forms of African American English. Educators may therefore need to pay particular attention to how African American English–speaking students pronounce and write future tense forms in standardized English.

Knowledge of how and why specific language variants appear in students' oral reading and writing is invaluable information when assessing students who speak African American English, because features of this variety will often appear in students' speech, oral reading, and written work. When pointing out students' grammatical mistakes, it is important to consider whether potential errors might actually be rooted in students' use of a language pattern characteristic of African American English. If so, it is important to explain the linguistic pattern to the student. This process entails pointing out to students their African American English–influenced pattern and, while acknowledging and appreciating this language variation, revealing how this pattern compares and contrasts with that of standardized English.

Above all, it is critical not to focus on identifying standardized English grammatical errors in students' speech, oral reading, and writing to the point that the quality of the content, organization, or style of the students' work is overlooked. As Smitherman-Donaldson (1987) noted, doing so overpenalizes African American English–speaking students who use features of their home language variety.

Challenges that are rooted in language variation are not only prevalent in the language arts classroom; they often surface in science and math classes as well. Although some may believe that learning mathematics is simply a question of manipulating numbers, in reality, some of the challenges that students encounter when they are asked to solve math word problems and written mathematical proofs are actually linguistic in nature (Abedi & Lord, 2001; Lager, 2006; Schleppegrell, 2007).

In math word problems, existential constructions such as *there is*, *there's*, and *there are* are frequently employed, as in such statements as "There are six apples in the bag." One difficulty for African American

English–speaking students may lie in the fact that the use of existential constructions varies in African American English, with *it is* and *it's* commonly used in place of *there is, there's,* and *there are*. These and similar types of variations may affect how African American English–speaking students read and process word problems.

Seeking further evidence of challenges that African American English–speaking students may face in math classrooms, Terry, Evangelou, and Smith (2009) examined the relationship between the linguistic complexity of word problems and students' success in carrying out the computation. In a study of 75 African American second-graders, Terry and colleagues estimated how each student's test performance was affected by two features of African American English: the absence of *-s* in third-person singular verb forms (as in "He talk a lot") and the absence of *-s* in possessive constructions (as in "My mama house is big"). The authors accounted for each student's overall ability and the difficulty of the math problem. For a core group of students, 9% more questions, on average, would have been answered correctly if the linguistic feature in question had not been included in the word problem. Terry and colleagues explain their results by suggesting that some African American English–speaking students may face an added cognitive load on their working memory when they read and process math word problems, due to language variation.

Issues concerning language variation relate to Abedi and Lord's (2001) finding that nonstandardized English–speaking students in the United States may perform 10% to 30% worse on math word problems than on comparable problems presented in a numeric format. These results indicate the significant role of linguistic factors in addition to computational skills.

Pitch, Tone, Rhythm, and Volume

The melody of speech includes pitch, tone, rhythm, and volume. Listeners may notice these features and perceive, for example, that a particular variety or language sounds fast, slow, high-pitched, or nasal. Although it is difficult to measure and describe these features, many listeners report that the melody and rhythm of a speaker's voice can mark that person as being African American, even if all other aspects of the person's language sound standardized (Baugh, 2000). Rhythmic patterns may also be preserved in speakers who do not use many of the more socially stigmatized sound, grammar, and vocabulary features of African American English.

Syllable stress. Speakers of African American English may stress the first syllable of words for which speakers of standardized English stress the second syllable. For example, the word *cement*, pronounced "ce-MENT" in standardized English usage, may be pronounced as "CE-ment" in African American English; *Detroit*, pronounced "de-TROIT" in standardized English, may be pronounced as "DE-troit" in African American English; and *umbrella*, pronounced "um-BRELL-a" in standardized English, may be pronounced as "UM-brell-a" in African American English. It is important to remember that these alternative syllable stress patterns are not random mispronunciations but rather are regular variations.

Pitch. Speakers of African American English may talk in a lower pitch than speakers of other varieties of English, although these findings have not been fully confirmed in linguistic research (Tarone, 1973; Wolfram & Thomas, 2002). Nevertheless, the use of deeper African American male voices in American media has left listeners with a perception of the African American male voice as deep and authoritative. For example, James Earl Jones is the voice of CNN and Dennis Haysbert is the voice of Allstate Auto Insurance. Several African American men have also portrayed God in popular movies, including Richard Pryor in *In God We Tru$t* (Feldman, 1980) and Morgan Freeman in *Bruce Almighty* (Shadyac, 2003).

Speakers of African American English also tend to have a wider pitch range and use more falsetto than speakers of standardized English (Cole, Thomas, Britt, & Coggshall, 2005; Jun & Foreman, 1996). Comedian Richard Pryor used falsetto for comic purposes, for example, while singers such as Little Richard and Prince often move from baritone to falsetto in their songs. In addition, speakers of African American English may use more pitch accents, and stressed syllables in particular may be uttered with a very high pitch.

Intonation. In standardized English, especially as used in the classroom, questions are generally expected to *rise* in their intonation. In the sentence "Are you going to the store?" the word *store* will usually be said with a rising intonation, whereas the other words in the sentence will usually be said with an intonation that is neither rising nor falling. In African American English, in contrast, questions may also be formed with *falling* or *flat* intonation. In this variety, the question "Are you going to the store?" may therefore be said with flat intonation (as in, "Are you going to the store"), without any words rising in their intonation or pitch.

Charity (2005) found a difference in the way that teachers asked questions in standardized English and the way that African American English–speaking students in several major cities imitated these questions. She gave a group of standardized English–speaking teachers the sentence "And then Joe asked, 'Isn't there any jelly?'" and asked them to pronounce it. Teachers' voices tended to rise at the end of the question, just as most questions asked in standardized English rise at the end.

When the African American English–speaking students repeated the sentence "And then Joe asked, 'Isn't there any jelly?'" their questions tended to not rise as high at the end as the teachers' questions did. In fact, many of the students asked the question with a nearly completely flat intonation. Differences in how questions are asked in African American English compared to standardized English can be critically important in how educators and peers perceive African American English–speaking students. Tone of voice matters, in school and in everyday interactions, because it is tied to notions of politeness, friendliness, and enthusiasm. Educators' knowledge of and respect for differences in students' use of intonation are extremely important when interpreting the emotional states of their students, including whether a student sounds polite, enthusiastic, respectful, bored, withdrawn, uncooperative, or angry.

Sometimes intonation patterns are misinterpreted. When intonation patterns that seem to signal negative emotions or behaviors, such as indifference or rudeness, interact with frequently misunderstood nonverbal behaviors, such as not making eye contact or shrugging one's shoulders, misimpressions of certain students may be intensified. In standardized English, the absence of a rise at the end of a question can be used to signal disengagement, lack of interest, and disrespect, but this is not the case in African American English, as speakers of this variety may produce questions that have rising, flat, or falling intonation patterns equally. If an African American student says "Why am I taking this test" (with a flat or falling intonation) versus "Why am I taking this test?" (with a rising intonation), the student's statement may be interpreted as a signal of aggression, uncooperativeness, noncompliance, withdrawal, or disrespect, even though the student may not have intended to send such a message.

In sum, based on whether students grew up speaking standardized English or African American English, variation in how they ask questions can lead to misunderstandings. The lack of melodic variation in the voices of African American students, especially male students, is often misinterpreted in a negative light and may be infused with perceptions of emotions that students do not mean to convey. As a result, African American English–speaking students may be improperly evaluated academically, socially, and emotionally.

Volume. Many stereotypes surround the idea that African Americans speak more loudly than other speakers, that African Americans tend to shout, and that African American students are more rambunctious than other students. At the same time, there also exists a paradoxical stereotype that African American English–speaking students are often silent or withdrawn. As a result, these students may be perceived as being standoffish, as sullen, as "having a wall up," and as being hard to get to know.

African American English–speaking students who do not talk much at school may also be perceived as having limited language skills. Evans-Winters (2005) described an African American girl named Zora, whose teachers thought she had a learning disability because she refused to talk while she was at school. As a result, Zora was asked to repeat first grade. Later, when she was in middle school, Zora explained that she had often felt nervous and out of place in school; she chose to not speak up in school settings both as a coping mechanism and as a way to avoid drawing attention to herself. Zora recalled that many teachers "thought I was slow, because I didn't say nothing when they asked me a question" (p. 101).

Classroom observations reveal that students who are less secure in adhering to the conventions of standardized English and who feel less safe in academic contexts may retreat into various stages of being quiet or what may be perceived as withdrawal. Other students may speak more loudly and behave in ways that are perceived as "acting out." These students may also use more features of African American English, shifting the style of what they are saying away from the standardized English that is generally expected in the school setting. Peers may even attempt to regulate or ridicule African American students' loud verbal performances, labeling them as "acting ghetto."

Educational implications. When working with African American English–speaking students who may not be confident in their use of standardized English and who may be engaging in verbal behaviors that vary from the language patterns that are expected to be used in school settings, it is important not to assume that variation in students' communication patterns signals low intelligence, uncooperativeness, or hostility. Rather, students may be using features of African American English to assert their identity. Students gain confidence and are able to enjoy academic and social success when they know and recognize academic English forms *and* when they recognize and value the language patterns they bring with them to school.

How educators react to African American English–speaking students' language variation sends an important message to these students about safety and acceptance. Positive messages help students view learning as an accessible and engaging process. Language differences can add to other school stressors; thus, the classroom must be a safe place in which to take risks and speak up if African American English–speaking students are to be willing to have their voices heard (Ball, 2000; Lee, 2006). Many complex linguistic and social issues must be taken into account to ensure African American English–speaking students' mental and emotional well-being in the classroom.

Conversation

Conversational norms in African American English may differ from those in other varieties of English in a few key ways, such as in how individuals greet each other. Whereas White children and adults may often use each other's first names to show friendship and familiarity, African American children and adults may prefer to use titles to show respect, both in situations in which there is a hierarchical difference between the speakers (e.g., doctor–patient or educator–student) and in situations that are more egalitarian (McNeely & Badami, 1984).

Conversational differences between standardized English and African American English may be easily misinterpreted. As Kochman (1981) pointed out, when members of different cultural groups assume that others are "operating according to identical speech and cultural conventions," when in fact different norms are in use, cross-cultural misunderstandings and conflict may occur (p. 8). A behavior that is often misinterpreted is the fact that African American students may make less eye contact than other students when listening to a speaker (Keulen et al., 1998).

Another example surrounds styles of turn-taking. When speaking with others, African American students may communicate in ways that are interactive and energetic, and they may engage in more conversational overlap, such that more than one person is speaking at a time (Day-Vines & Day-Hairston, 2005). Overlapping with another speaker is often viewed as normal and comfortable in African American English and in other varieties, such as Jewish American English (Schiffrin, 1984, 1994).

In standardized English, overlap may be considered a form of interruption and may be offensive to the speaker, but some students adhere to different conversational norms. Morakinyo (1995) found that due to African American students' use of overlapping turns, educators perceived these students as being boisterous, loud, and out of control. It is important to be sensitive to variations in how students converse with each other and with educators. If the conversational norms of standardized English are expected, then these conventions may need to be explicitly taught.

Storytelling. The narration styles that African American English speakers use may vary significantly from the style that is used in standardized English. Michaels (1981) found that African American students, and African American girls in particular, were more likely to tell narratives in a "topic-associating" style, in which a series of topics, anecdotes, or episodes may be presented to the listener. The topics are related by a common theme, although this relationship may not be made explicit to the listener, and the topics may not be presented in a linear way with a clear beginning, middle, and end. This style differs from the more directly linear, single-topic narrative style that is considered normative in standardized English.

Michaels (1981) reported that the teacher in the specific classroom that was studied had difficulty seeing the relevance of students' stories when they were told in the topic-associating style. The teacher often had trouble predicting the direction of these students' stories and would frequently make comments or ask questions in ways that interrupted the students' train of thought and narrative flow. The teacher even became frustrated on some occasions, asking that students keep their storytelling "important" and that their stories deal with "one thing only."

Michaels and Cazden (1986) further confirmed that the topic-associating style of storytelling is perceived negatively when it is inconsistent with what educators expect. Educators may assume that students understand how to tell a story in a certain way, according to a model that they have in their minds, but the structure of the model may be unfamiliar to students and may not have been made explicit to them. Michaels and Cazden also found that educators who did not understand the topic-associating style of storytelling were more likely to interrupt African American students compared with White students during circle-time and sharing-time activities. Such interruptions by educators can lead to confusion and frustration for students who do not understand the source of the mismatches between their own communication styles and the expectations that educators have of them (Labov, 1972; Piestrup, 1973).

Scholars have also found that differences in storytelling styles may negatively affect the educational assessment of young students. Reid and Valle (2004) noted that children who tell stories in ways that do not conform to the normative style expected in school settings may be perceived to lack those preliteracy skills that are deemed to be necessary for so-called kindergarten readiness.

Given these variations, students may need to be taught, for example, that sometimes stories have only one central topic and that it may be important to point out relationships between different topics for some listeners to understand the story's coherence. It is also necessary to recognize the different types of storytelling styles that students may use and to understand that narrating in a topic-associating style is a linguistic difference, not a cognitive or linguistic deficiency. Respect for and understanding of cultural differences in storytelling styles among students and peers should be established, and it is important for all students to be given space to tell stories in ways that are comfortable to them. Educators can provide all students with the understanding and respect they need to appreciate stories that are told in a variety of styles.

STRATEGIES FOR EDUCATORS

Educators may teach all students about language diversity by instructing them about oration and rhetoric. Educators may invite guest speakers to tell stories or read aloud from literature written in African American English, and students may compose work modeled after what they have heard. Students may also examine rhetorical styles used in African American speeches and sermons by such orators as Martin Luther King Jr. and President Barack Obama, considering what social and personal reasons might have led these speakers to develop their styles.

Goodman (2003) recommended that all students be encouraged to read different texts and talk about the language variation they find in them. For younger readers, books that include dialogue in African American English are *My Brother Fine with Me* (Clifton, 1975), *Flossie and the Fox* (McKissack, 1986), and *The Tales of Uncle Remus* (Lester, 1987). Older students may enjoy reading works by popular African American authors including Zora Neale Hurston and Ralph Ellison. Similarly, Hudson (1993) suggested using dialogue and first-person narratives in fiction as a means to illustrate language variation, and Lee (2007) described how to use diverse discourse styles as a resource for classroom instruction.

Direct versus indirect commands. Indirect commands are common in standardized English, especially in the School English used in educational settings. For example, students may be asked to form a line through the use of indirect statements such as "Let's get lined up," "I don't see anyone standing in line yet," or "I like the way some of you are standing in line." In African American English, however, it is common to use direct commands, such as "I want you to line up now." African American English–speaking students therefore may interpret indirect commands that are couched in politeness strategies as preferences or suggestions rather than commands, and they may therefore choose not to obey. Educators may wish to explicitly teach an awareness of different cultural norms surrounding suggestions and commands. For example, educators may explain that "Let's get lined up" and "I like the way you all are talking quietly" may carry the same meanings as "Line up now" and "Please talk quietly."

In a similar vein, African American English–speaking educators may issue more direct commands to their students, such as "I want you to line up now" or "Stop talking." It is important to be mindful that these educators are not necessarily being harsh with their students but rather may be operating according to different cultural and linguistic norms surrounding the use of direct versus indirect speech.

Verbal play. Forms of verbal play have been well documented in research on African American English, including the ways that African American English–speaking students interact with peers. *Instigation,* or the initiation of spoken commentary or insult in order to provoke response, is one communication tactic through which African American English speakers go on the verbal offensive. The form of verbal jousting known variously as *signifying, joaning,* and *playing the dozens* is similar to instigation, though it is generally more playful. In this form of ritualized verbal play, opponents exchange insults, usually about each other or about members of the other person's family. So-called "yo mama jokes" are one form of signifying that has been popularized in the media. While such jokes may sound offensive, the jokes are also vehicles through which African American English–speaking students make use of figurative language, draw on shared cultural and personal knowledge, and learn verbal and creative improvisation skills similar to the skills that are built when artists learn to "improv" in jazz music or to "freestyle" in rap and hip-hop music. The danger with instigation and signifying is that playful teasing may be misinterpreted, and it may segue into other forms of confrontation. Verbal confrontation at school may lead to conflict, which may cause a student to be reprimanded or punished. Knowledge of the rituals of verbal jousting may be important when assessing whether or not students are engaging in verbal play.

Hyperbole. In hyperbole, speakers engage in exaggerated or grandiose accounts or evaluations of their own behavior or personal characteristics. In athletics, such bravado may manifest itself in boasting, such as Muhammad Ali's claim "I am the greatest," which, while very likely true in retrospect, was interpreted by many people at the time as a grandiose boast. Other examples of athletic bravado include engaging in creative and personalized dance routines after making a touchdown in football. Hyperbolic statements and behavior may be seen by some critics as being at odds with notions of "good sportsmanship," in which boasting is viewed as antagonistic toward those who did not perform as well and high-performing athletes and teams are expected to at least somewhat downplay their achievements.

African American English–speaking students may be reprimanded for the use of hyperbole because it may be perceived as harmful boasting that fosters competition among students, mocks the lesser abilities of other students, and provokes conflict among students. It is important to remember the cultural roots of hyperbole and displays of grandeur and to realize that these features are aspects of verbal play. Educators can discuss these verbal tactics with students, explaining when such forms have their use and when they might offend others, particularly those from different cultural backgrounds.

Vocabulary

Many new words have come into American English through the speech of African Americans. Exclusive vocabulary and expressions were once a powerful means of resistance for enslaved Africans brought to North America, who often used words or phrases that were unintelligible to their owners. In fact, spirituals often used coded language to discuss such sensitive matters as escape. Smitherman (1986) noted that lyrics such as "steal away to Jesus" sometimes meant "stealing away from the plantation to freedom"; "this train is bound for Glory" sometimes referred to the "freedom train" that ran on the symbolic Underground Railroad; and "Go down, Moses" sometimes referred to freedom fighter Harriet Tubman, who would "go down South" to tell plantation owners to "let her people go" (p. 48).

Major (1994) provided an overview of how the African American English lexicon developed historically. Many terms that originated in African American English have become widespread, such as *jazz, jive,* and *hip,* which stem from African American music traditions. African American English also contains vocabulary items that are not commonly used by speakers of standardized English, such as *saditty* (snobby or pretentious), *kitchen* (curly hair at the nape of the neck), and *in a minute* (for a while, as in "I haven't seen him in a minute" for "I haven't seen him in a while") (Major, 1994).

The overwhelming popularity of typically African American music styles, such as R&B, rap, and hip-hop, has brought wider recognition of words that originated in African American English. Just as early jazz musicians coined terms that have been adopted into general usage, rap and hip-hop artists have produced new terms as well. The *Urban Dictionary* (2009), edited by everyday readers, contains some of the most contemporary vocabulary available. For example, the words *yo*, *young'un*, and *shorty* (pronounced "SHO-ty" or "SHAW-ty") may be used in casual conversation to both address and refer to a male or female young person (as in "Yo is a clown!" and "Where you been, shorty?"). In addition, because African American English is often perceived as being *cool* (a term that originated in African American English), its vocabulary and phrases are often used in advertising. Many African American English phrases, such as "you go, girl," "you the man," "off the hook," and "that's the bomb," have been popularized in the media and have come into use by the general public.

Individual Variability

Many features of African American English that we have discussed have been described and analyzed in relation to speakers across the United States. At the same time, differences have been reported in the frequency of use of African American English features on the basis of social differences in age, gender, region, social class, and other dimensions.

Craig and Washington (2002, 2004) studied lower- and middle-class preschoolers, kindergartners, and first-graders enrolled in Detroit area public schools. They found that, at school entry, African American boys and African American students from lower-income homes tended to use features of African American English more often than African American girls and African American students from middle-income homes. These significant differences, however, disappeared in later grades. Furthermore, Craig and Washington (2004, 2006) found that, for most African American English–speaking students, a shift tended to occur between kindergarten and third grade, during which time most of the students reduced their use of African American English features by more than half. Those students who decreased their use of African American English features between kindergarten and fifth grade were found to have higher reading achievement scores, whereas those students who did not become well versed in standardized English forms by fourth or fifth grade typically ended up one or more grade levels behind. The effects of learning to use standardized English forms or not learning to do so thus have serious and early effects on students' school success. Craig and Washington suggested that it is not the initial language variety that students bring with them to school but rather institutional responses to their language differences that ultimately lead to nonstandardized English–speaking students' academic failure.

Craig, Thompson, Washington, and Potter (2003) and Craig and Washington (2004) also researched the frequency with which individual students used African American English and found a great deal of variability in how often features were used. Craig and colleagues (2003) found that African American elementary students doing a read-aloud exercise used, on average, one feature of African American English per 20 words. At the same time, Craig and Washington (2004) found that some of the students they studied used no features of African American English at all, while others used a great deal of them. Kindergartners in Craig and Washington's (2004) study ranged from using as many as one feature of African American English per 4 words to as few as one feature per 91 words. The first- through fifth-graders in their study ranged from using as many as one feature of African American English per 5 words to no features of African American English at all.

With respect to gender, studies from linguistics and developmental psychology suggest that girls tend to develop language earlier than boys, which lends some credence to the common belief in the United States that girls are more verbal than boys (Charity Hudley, 2008). This finding must be interpreted with caution, however, since it does not extend as a general rule across cultures, and it is important to remember that individual girls and boys can be very different in their language development. Nevertheless, this general finding can be a rule of thumb for understanding how girls and boys in the United States often develop language skills.

Other general findings with respect to gender include evidence that suggests male speakers tend to use more nonstandardized forms than their female peers do, although this pattern most often holds true in the United States and similar societies and does not extend across all cultures (Eckert & McConnell-Ginet, 2003). At the same time, a somewhat contradictory finding exists. Girls and women may be more resistant to using language features that are stigmatized by others, but when it comes to using new features, girls and women are more often innovators, whose use of new features often helps spur and spread language change (Labov, 2001).

Linguistic variation is partially responsible for some gender-based patterns of interaction in school settings. More than three-fourths of all teachers are women (Corcoran, Evans, & Schwab, 2004). The overrepresentation of women educators may benefit female students, whose communication patterns may be closer to those of the women who are often supervising and instructing them. Female students may also be more sensitive to language instruction that is modeled by female teachers, and therefore girls may learn standardized English forms more quickly. Female educators are also likely to have certain notions about what is polite and acceptable that may be informed by their own standpoints and worldviews as women. As a result, female educators may perceive that girls are easier to work with than boys, since girls' language and behavior may be closer to the style that female educators privilege in the classroom (Peterson & Kennedy, 2006).

Nevertheless, girls are often held to stricter linguistic standards than boys. Verbal disruptions such as cursing, arguing, interrupting teachers, blurting out answers, asking many questions, and teasing are some behaviors that tend to conflict with the gendered norms and expectations that educators have of their female students (Eckert & McConnell-Ginet, 2003). It is therefore important not to reprimand girls disproportionately for verbal behaviors that run counter to educators' expectations, which may risk silencing girls' voices and negatively affect their engagement with and participation in school settings.

In another explanation as to why boys' and girls' language use may differ, Ferguson (2001) suggested that boys might miss some of their female educators' verbal cues in their formative years by paying more attention instead to the language of their male peers. Many conflicts in schools are due to verbal behaviors and miscommunications between educators and male students. Especially in primary schools, the general lack of men as K–12 educators leaves boys without gender-specific linguistic role models at the very time when language patterns are being taught and become ingrained.

African American boys may face additional linguistic and behavioral challenges related to discipline and attention since educators may view them as being aggressive troublemakers before they even misbehave (Ferguson, 2001; Grant, 2004). African American boys continue to have disproportionately higher rates of being placed into special education courses and speech therapy programs and higher rates of suspension and expulsion than African American girls (Cartledge & Dukes, 2008; Harry & Anderson, 1995). Some of this context may explain why African American girls tend to achieve much better on some educational measures than African American boys. Banks and Banks (2004) noted that on the verbal sections of the SAT, boys outperform girls across all races and ethnicities, with one exception: African American girls earn higher verbal scores than African American boys. In addition, African American girls are about twice as likely as African American boys to take Advanced Placement exams.

African American girls still face their own educational challenges. Grant (2004) found that educators often ask African American girls to run errands for them and that educators often focus on improving the social skills and manners of African American girls, who are perceived as being overly loud and aggressive. Morris (2007) found in his study of elementary school classrooms that educators often explicitly said they wanted to encourage their African American female students to become more "ladylike" and docile so that they would not learn to be "loud" or to "challenge authority" (p. 501). Indeed, some educators may hold paradoxical perceptions about the behavior of African American girls, who may be viewed as being silent and passive as well as loud and confrontational (Fordham, 1993). Due to differences in communicative norms and cultural misunderstandings, the status of being a "good student" may remain difficult for African American girls to attain.

THE TAKE-AWAY MESSAGE

With knowledge and understanding of African American English, educators have a greater appreciation for the communication patterns and rich linguistic heritages of their African American English–speaking students. Linguistically informed educators are also better equipped to instruct African American English–speaking students in ways that enable them to recognize and value the rules, norms, and conventions of standardized English while also recognizing and valuing the language patterns they bring with them from home.

Throughout this chapter, we have presented information and practical strategies for educators of African American English–speaking students, but more research is still needed to fully examine these students' linguistic and educational experiences. We are working with educators to further design pedagogically sound and linguistically informed strategies to help students navigate between the types and meanings of African American English forms and those of standardized English in their oral reading, writing, and speech. In working to meet these goals, linguists and educators can support the educational attainment of African American English–speaking students as we continue to build our knowledge base about language variation and change within diverse U.S. schools.

5

Assessment and Application

TESTING AND ACCOUNTABILITY are prevalent across educational environments, as educators seek to measure what students have learned and what they can learn. As educators ourselves, we understand the importance of assessment at all educational levels. Assessments may determine which students receive extra attention, such as being included in gifted and talented programs and receiving scholarships based on achievement and/or aptitude. Assessments may also be used to track the progress of schools, as educators and administrators may be held responsible for the scores of a class, a district, or an entire school system. In school systems, the amount of funding that a school receives can sometimes be tied to the test scores of the school's student population.

In this chapter, we explore key linguistic issues related to standardized tests and other assessments that students face in educational settings. Language-related issues rooted in test design and test preparation can be major contributors to systematic differences in test scores and educational achievement for students who speak nonstandardized varieties of English. Knowledge of how language variation can affect the assessment of nonstandardized English–speaking students is critical for educators, both as they assess their own students and as they help their students prepare for the many types of standardized tests they encounter throughout their school careers.

When examining the fairness of testing models and addressing the cultural biases that some tests contain, it is necessary to keep the goals of standardized testing in mind. Standardized tests measure students' aptitude and achievement against a set of objectives and against the results of other students' performance. Aptitude tests are designed to predict future performance, and as such they tend not to cover information that was directly taught in specific curricula. Many aptitude tests are not as accurate and reliable in their predictions of future performance as they are expected to be. Alon and Tienda (2007) recommended that universities concentrate on high school grade point average and class rank in admissions decisions, since these measures have been shown to be as good as if not better than standardized aptitude test scores as predictors of college success.

Achievement tests, in contrast, are intended to measure what the test taker learned in a particular subject area as directly taught in a curriculum. Achievement tests are based on the assumption that the material being tested has been delivered to all test takers in an equitable way. Yet inequalities in education often violate these assumptions that standardized achievement tests make regarding the equality of exposure to instruction and opportunities for learning in the test population.

TESTING SPECIFIC POPULATIONS

Much social commentary has surrounded the ways that standardized assessments, which determine much of students' educational and occupational successes, may be culturally biased. When there are inequalities in the educational system, underprivileged students and students from cultural groups that have historically not received full access to education tend to disproportionately feel their impact. The basic concept of measuring deviation from the norm that is central to test development puts nonstandardized English–speaking test takers at a disadvantage, since such students are never the norm. Some of these cultural groups include students of lower socioeconomic status, Southern students, and African American students.

Testing Students of Lower Socioeconomic Status

There are many resource issues related to testing students of lower socioeconomic status. The disproportionate allocation of wealth in the United States allows some schools to be better funded than others and allows parents with high socioeconomic status to send their children to better public or private schools (Feagin, Vera, & Imani, 1996; Oliver & Shapiro, 1995). Resources at privileged schools are more concentrated, and classes are smaller. In this way, educational advantages are transferred from wealthier parents to their children (Feagin et al., 1996; Roscigno, 1998).

Many students of lower socioeconomic status attend schools where resources are scarce, and their classrooms may have high rates of overcrowding. Overcrowding, in particular, can cause distractions and hinder concentration when students are taking tests, as unruly behavior, outside noise, and other disturbances do not always cease at test time. Other issues related to economics, such as poor nutrition and sleep habits, may present further challenges for students of lower socioeconomic status. Such factors are often not taken into account when standardized tests are given and when they are validated, often leaving students and educators to blame for disparities in test scores that they cannot alleviate.

An additional challenge is that students of lower socioeconomic status, who may also be students from historically underserved cultural groups, tend to be disproportionately tracked into lower-level classes in ways that do not always reflect their actual academic abilities (Oakes, 1987; Persell, 2007). These inequalities can begin in kindergarten, when placement in higher-ability classes and/or gifted and talented programs, as well as in remedial classes and/or special education programs, is often determined. At the secondary level, students of lower socioeconomic status are much more likely to be tracked into average classes or into vocational programs, and they are much less likely to take honors classes, Advanced Placement (AP) classes, and International Baccalaureate (IB) classes, which provide important preparation for standardized aptitude tests, such as the SAT, and for college. For many students of lower socioeconomic status who attend schools with fewer resources, AP and IB programs are not even offered. Thus, on the basis of economic factors, many students are fundamentally disadvantaged.

Scholars have recognized that disparities in the investments that economically diverse groups of parents and guardians make in their children's school success strongly influence whether or not their children succeed in high school and attend college (Charles, Roscigno, & Torres, 2007). Part of this process requires that parents understand the significance of the standardized tests that students may take. Parents who have not been to college themselves may also not understand the importance of taking certain tests like the SAT more than once to get the best score, particularly since it is commonly believed that these tests cannot be studied for.

Some parents also may not understand the importance of school assessments or tests required for graduation. One principal who spoke with Anne relayed his dismay at the fact that one of the best African American students at his school had to sit out a year after high school because the student did not take the proper standardized tests required by the college he wished to attend (Charity Hudley, 2009). The school counselor had missed the fact that this student had not taken the tests, and his parents, not having been to college themselves, did not know which tests were required. Often, parents who are unfamiliar with the college application process trust that their children will get the assistance they need from educators. As revealed in this story, however, not only academically struggling students but also students who are at the top of their classes need guidance on their way to educational and occupational success.

Students of lower socioeconomic status, who may speak and write in a manner that disadvantages them on standardized tests from the start, also often need access to the tips and techniques that test preparation classes provide but may not receive these services. As Cole (1995) noted, standardized test coaching and preparation is a multimillion-dollar industry, despite the fact that many test developers insist that the nature of standardized aptitude tests makes them unable to be studied for in such a manner. Lower-income parents may have fewer resources to invest in pretest preparations such as training courses and online test-preparation materials, and they may not understand why money should be spent in this way. In addition, test preparation courses and tutoring services may not be available for free or as a part of the regular curriculum at these students' schools as they are at schools with greater resources, and thus students of lower socioeconomic status are at a further disadvantage.

Even if students of lower socioeconomic status have access to test-prep materials or tutors, these resources may not address the subtle linguistic differences that, for nonstandardized English–speaking test takers, are crucial factors in achieving test success. One solution for addressing these concerns may lie in establishing connections between universities and high schools. Partnerships may be arranged to provide tutoring and test-prep services for underprivileged students, particularly in the absence of funding for students to attend commercial test-preparation courses.

Testing Southern Students

In general, Southern students have not been well studied as a test-taking population, and relatively little research has explored differences in test scores between Southerners and other populations. In one report, Lemann (1995) described an aptitude test that was developed in 1950: Male college students who scored high enough on the test would be eligible for draft deferment. In 1951, the Educational Testing Service (ETS) examined data from this test, and "what leaped out from the results was the substantial regional differences in the pass rates: 73 percent of college students in New England made a 70 or above, but only 42 percent in the Deep South did" (Lemann, 1995, para. 49). As

Lemann noted, fortunately for ETS and unfortunately for the Southern male college students who were less likely to do well, the validity of the draft-deferment test was not challenged.

The South still lags behind other regions of the United States in overall educational achievement on several measures (Suitts, 2007). Results from the mathematical assessment of the 2009 National Assessment of Educational Progress, given to fourth- and eighth-grade students, revealed large gaps in scores by racial or ethnic group and also by state: In Massachusetts, 57% of fourth-graders scored at or above "proficient" on the test, while only 16% of students in Mississippi did so (National Center for Education Statistics, 2009). As William Schmidt, a professor of education, was quoted as saying, "How can we as a nation allow such disparity?" (Dillon, 2009).

In grades K–12, Southern students from lower-income backgrounds are put in special education classes at higher rates than students from other regions of the United States, and they have higher rates of illiteracy (Suitts, 2007). Scholars have also explored how poverty and related social factors affect young Southern students with respect to the early literacy–language interface (Dickinson, Darrow, & Tinubu, 2008; Kainz & Vernon-Feagans, 2007; Morrison & Connor, 2009). Beyond K–12, research finds that Southern students from lower-income backgrounds are less likely to attend college than comparable students from the rest of the nation. The South has the highest percentage of persons 25 years of age and older without a high school diploma and the lowest rates of adults who have earned a college degree (Suitts, 2007).

Economic factors such as higher rates of poverty, low family income and wealth, and low expenditures per K–12 pupil all affect education in the South. Smaller school budgets and overcrowded classrooms may translate into poorer conditions for learning, less educator time spent with students, and less school funding for extra materials, including new books, computer labs, science equipment, field trips, tutoring programs, and test-prep courses.

Despite such challenges, it is important to remember that top-quality educational experiences have been and continue to be offered by schools and educators throughout the South. Because we attended Southern schools ourselves, we recognize and acknowledge the strengths of the educations we received there. Nevertheless, because Southern schools tend to have fewer resources to distribute across a growing and increasingly diversifying student population, Southern students are often hit disproportionately hard. These difficulties represent significant adversities that educators and students in the South continue to face.

Testing African American Students

In the history of the United States, African Americans have faced many educational inequalities (Anderson, 1988). Until 1972, African Americans and all other non-Whites were excluded from the standardization sample of the Stanford-Binet test. As such, these groups were left out of the development of the standardized tests that were designed to identify who was bright and who could move up the rungs of the social and economic ladder.

Several issues particularly affect African American students as a test-taking population. Racial characterizations of test takers are often absolute; although the changing climate surrounding racial identification in the United States may provide for some exceptions, it is generally the case that each test taker is defined as a member of one racial group or classified as "other." In the United States, individuals having "one drop" of blood from a line of African descent have historically been considered to be African American. This method of racial classification for African Americans contrasts with methods of classification for Native Americans, Latinos, and other racial and ethnic groups. For example, Native American classification policies center on the individual having enough Native American heritage to claim tribal membership. Even so, in the past, having "too much" African American heritage was taken into account as well. In the early 1900s, persons with one-fourth African American ancestry or more were deemed ineligible for official Native American tribal membership (Blankenship, 1998).

The impact of the different ways that students may be racially classified is, in part, a question of test validity. If it is difficult to determine what racial group a student belongs to, or if racial classification systems that are known to be inaccurate continue to be used, then analysis and reporting of the test results along racial and ethnic lines may be called into question. When test results are presented by race, economic differences within racial groups may not be well accounted for. Impoverished and working-class African American students do not always have the same social and educational opportunities as middle-class and upper-class African American students, yet both groups take the same tests. Overgeneralized reports may discuss test scores by students' race in ways that suggest misleading interpretations.

In the past, psychologists and anthropologists have used IQ tests to try to establish links among race (particularly for African Americans), brain size, intelligence, social behaviors, and personality traits. Although the idea that a person's race affects his or her IQ has been roundly disproved, the history of testing in the United States is tainted with racial biases (Fischer et al., 1996; Lemann, 1999). Issues of IQ assessment can even be questions of life or death, as IQ test scores are used to determine if defendants have sufficient mental capacity to legally be executed for capital crimes (*Atkins v. Virginia*, 2002).

Many people still hold onto beliefs that African American students are naturally not as smart as White or Asian students. Such beliefs are not only patently false but also destructive, as they prop up detrimental stereotypes and lead to lowered expectations for African American students. Indeed, negative social stereotypes and lower racial expectations have been shown to severely affect African American test takers on a psychological level. Steele and Aronson (1995) found that African American students at Stanford University were more likely than comparable White peers to experience test anxiety and underestimate their own performance on tests. For tests that include a verbal component, conventional testing situations have been shown to cause African American students to become hesitant and taciturn (Labov, 1972) or to perform less well than their ability level would predict (Steele & Aronson, 1995). These factors may significantly affect how well African American students perform on standardized tests. Because test takers' scores may vary according to their psychological or emotional state, standardized tests may have more measurement error when it comes to African American students' scores, yet these lower test scores are often taken at face value and are used as the basis for many decisions that are then made about these students, educationally as well as socially.

The federal judiciary has, to some extent, recognized the unfair nature of IQ tests. For instance, courts have rejected efforts to use IQ tests as the sole determinant of whether a student should be placed in special education classes, given the tests' racially disparate impact (*Larry P. v. Riles*, 1984). In the lower court's opinion in *Larry P. v. Riles* (1979), Judge Robert Peckham characterized the standardized intelligence tests at issue in that case as being

> racially and culturally biased, hav[ing] a discriminatory impact against black children, and hav[ing] not been validated for the purpose of essentially permanent placements of black children into educationally dead-end, isolated, and stigmatizing classes for the so-called educable mentally retarded. (p. 933)

Special education programs themselves have also occasionally been used to segregate students on the basis of race, ethnicity, and socioeconomic status (Lazerson, 1983).

Knowledge about the inequitable history of assessment may increase the stress that African American students, educators, parents, and guardians may feel toward test taking. African Americans of all ages may devalue, be suspicious of, or have high levels of anxiety surrounding assessment, particularly when it is known that tests can inaccurately represent the aptitude and achievements of African Americans. For example, when Charity (2007) studied the language patterns of 4- and 5-year-old African American children in several cities around the United States, she discovered that many African American children were worried that just talking with her would somehow cause them to be held back a grade if they did not do a good job in the conversations.

With respect to high school–aged youth, Hanson (2009) also found that African American girls, who often show an interest in and aptitude for science and math that is greater than their White counterparts, nevertheless face serious educational barriers, including cultural and linguistic biases on standardized tests and educators' negative stereotypes about their potential for achievement. These factors can hinder African American girls' success in high school and diminish their aspirations for success in college. African American students deserve to feel that school is not a place where they are under surveillance and at risk of failure, but rather an environment that fosters their learning and in which educators are striving to help them succeed.

Kozol (2005) summarized the various social outcomes of the intersection of wealth, race, education, and intelligence testing as follows: Students who are poor and go to racially and economically segregated schools often score lower on standardized tests, end up taking fewer subjects, and are offered fewer opportunities in school. Poorer schools with fewer resources continue to receive fewer resources due to their student body's low performance on standardized tests. In many areas, schools can also lose their autonomy when standardized test scores dip too low, with the state government stepping in to take over from local officials. While this system may make some educators and administrators achieve more, many others feel they are being punished unfairly, since the forces that cause their students to face disparate challenges have not been addressed and rectified.

THE CULTURE OF STANDARDIZED TESTS

As described by McIntosh (1988), some privileged students come to school carrying what she calls "special provisions" in the form of mainstream cultural knowledge. This cultural information, while necessary for academic success in mainstream classrooms, is not readily acquired at school, which leaves students from other backgrounds at a disadvantage.

Popham (2001) summarized the inequality, stating, "[On] traditionally constructed standardized achievement tests, many of the items . . . measure things that children bring to school. They measure how smart a kid is when he walked through the door, and not what he was supposed to learn in that school" (para. 41).

The cultural information that some students bring with them to school can affect their scores on many educational measures, particularly reading comprehension questions. Reading comprehension is widely considered difficult to measure by test makers and educators alike. Two main types of questions are used to assess comprehension of a reading passage. *Passage-dependent* questions can only be answered correctly by using information from the text, as in the question "What time did the girl in the story eat dinner?" *Passage-independent* questions can be answered by using information the reader already knows, as in the question "What color is the broccoli?"

For some students, the social and cultural information they bring with them to the test enables them to answer more questions as passage-independent. In other words, these students are more able to rely on personal cultural knowledge rather than having to carefully read the text, which may save them a few crucial minutes of test-taking time. In contrast, students whose social and cultural knowledge differs from that of the test makers, including students of lower socioeconomic status and students from historically underserved cultural groups, may experience a greater number of test questions as being passage-dependent. These students, who have to rely more on assessing information that is presented in the passage, may be slowed down on the test, while students who already have a cultural background that is more likely to be incorporated into test material and test questions may have a distinct advantage.

For example, one commonly used sixth-grade literacy test asked students to read and answer questions from a passage about yoga. Although anyone can practice this form of exercise, marketing strategies have made yoga particularly attractive to White, middle-class women in the United States (Strauss, 2005). Students, particularly those whose family members or other adult role models practice yoga or who, for whatever reason, are already familiar with yoga-specific vocabulary words and phrases that the passage contains, may have a far easier time decoding and comprehending this reading passage. For other students who are less familiar with yoga, reading about this topic may be more difficult. For these students, much more of the information is passage-dependent, and the meanings of specialized vocabulary items, such as *tone, poses, postures, squatting,* and *standing leg,* may be less immediately clear. Students who have to read and reread the passage carefully to understand the content or who have to pause over new words and infer their meaning from context may lose precious extra minutes on timed standardized tests compared to students who are already familiar with the subject matter and may be able to skim the text.

Sometimes reading comprehension passages assess culturally specific interpretations of morality, despite the fact that they purportedly assess comprehension. In a reading passage that was included in one Northeastern state's assessment test, a story is told about a son who makes a mess in his family's kitchen by baking a cake for his mother while she is out for the day. A comprehension question about the reading passage asks test takers to give their opinion as to whether the boy's mother will be upset, happy, or angry when she comes home and sees the state of the kitchen and the cake that her son made. The correct answer, according to the test, is that the mother's joy at seeing the cake will override her annoyance or anger that her son has messed up her kitchen. Of course, this answer relies on many cultural and moral assumptions. Test items that are based on questions of perceived morality thus entail inherent biases for test takers whose social, cultural, and moral values may differ from what test makers had in mind.

Many states also have end-of-grade tests designed to assess K–12 student achievement across various subjects. In the state of Virginia, the Virginia Standards of Learning (SOL) tests "represent a broad consensus of what parents, classroom teachers, school administrators, academics, and business and community leaders believe schools should teach and students should learn" (Virginia Department of Education, n.d.). The SOLs contain both multiple-choice and extended-response questions, and students must pass the tests to graduate from high school. Rubrics are given online, and teachers are provided materials and continuing education to help them teach the curriculum and administer the tests.

As on the previously discussed test, in which a story is told about a son who makes a mess by baking a cake for his mother while she is away, some narratives used on the Virginia SOLs are built around certain values. Test questions often center on the value of sharing; the value of standing out and apart from others, especially from family members; and the value of working together. Not all students take tests with the same values in mind. In particular, students may hold different, culturally based beliefs about the value of individuality compared to the value of more communal or collaborative behavior.

Many stories on the Virginia SOLs emphasize the value of history and tradition, especially that of Virginia. Traditional stories that include information about American culture and history presume that students have been exposed to certain cultural themes. Students who just moved to the area are often at a particular disadvantage when faced with this type of localized testing, as are students who have not had the advantage of visiting many historical sites in Virginia that are prominently featured on the test, such as Williamsburg, Jamestown, and Monticello. Other state tests may pose similar challenges for specific groups of students.

In response to calls for standardized tests to reflect greater sensitivity to the diversity of the test-taking population, some test makers are striving to include more passages on tests that deal with multicultural themes and issues. These types of passages are intended to level the playing field by providing situations for which different students—not only students from White cultures, from mainstream backgrounds, or with middle-class sensibilities—will have familiarity with the subject matter at hand. Sometimes, however, best intentions may not yield desired results. For example, one common standardized test included a reading passage on Kwanzaa. The passage explained that the holiday is celebrated by African Americans and serves to remind people who celebrate it of the ways that the first African Americans lived. The passage describes decorating with the colors black, red, and green to represent Kwanzaa, as well as eating specific foods, including chicken, catfish, greens, corn bread, and sweet potato pie.

It is true that the subject of Kwanzaa is relatively benign in nature and representative of a positive aspect of African American culture. Yet African American students are not all familiar with Kwanzaa just because they are African American, and few African Americans celebrate the holiday with the diligence that is suggested in the reading passage. It is therefore not necessarily the case that African American students will be more likely than students from other cultural backgrounds to draw on information about Kwanzaa in a passage-independent way. In fact, the reading passage makes many generalizations about African American practices and implies that the family who is described as celebrating Kwanzaa is representative of all African Americans. As we have noted, the process of taking tests that include stereotypes about African American culture has been found to lead to anxiety for African American students and lower their performance on standardized tests (Steele, 1992; Steele & Aronson, 1995).

THE LANGUAGE OF STANDARDIZED TESTS

In Chapter 2, we adapted McIntosh's (1988) metaphor to introduce the idea of the standardized English privileges that some students bring with them to school in the form of "invisible dictionaries." Some students come to school already possessing important cultural as well as linguistic knowledge that helps them succeed in academic settings. Privileged students who come to school already knowing dominant cultural references as well as the conventions of School English, including how to appropriately address educators, how to ask questions, how to take turns, and how to respond to known-answer questions, are already a step ahead. When it comes to taking tests, a preexisting knowledge of standardized English also allows some students to be multiple steps ahead of others who are not already carrying invisible dictionaries in their invisible knapsacks (see also Snow, Burns, & Griffin, 1998). Privileged students who are already familiar with the type of standardized English used on standardized tests will be far better test takers and may, as a result, be afforded more educational opportunities.

The language of standardized tests consists of the features of School English and standardized English from Chapter 2 and largely excludes nonstandardized English variants, such as those found in Chapters 3 and 4. As a result, nonstandardized English–speaking students may be disadvantaged in testing situations that depend on the use of standardized English. Hoover, Politzer, and Taylor (1995) categorized the different types of linguistic biases that may affect such students. They focused on variations in pronunciation, such as vowel mergers and consonant cluster reduction; variations in grammatical forms, such as the absence of helping and linking forms of the verb *to be* and the use of *was* for *were*; variations in pitch, tone, rhythm, and volume; and variations in conversational style and vocabulary. We focus on many of these issues below.

Sound

On standardized tests, pronunciation patterns may be tested in various ways, including the writing of letter sounds, word identification, sound-spelling correspondence, and oral reading fluency. Some of these assessments overpenalize nonstandardized English–speaking students.

One challenge is that assessments may conflate age-related language differences with language variation. For example, the production of *th* sounds in standardized English (e.g., in *birthday*) does not solidify in young speakers until age 6 or 7. Speakers of African American English may variably produce *th* sounds (e.g., "birfday" for *birthday*) not just in childhood but throughout their lives. Parents, educators, speech pathologists, and other professionals who do not have an accurate understanding of language variation may misdiagnose students who speak African American English as being developmentally challenged or delayed.

Some contemporary aptitude and achievement tests, especially those designed to assess the aptitude of beginning readers, have responded to language variation by including a caveat in the test's directions that instructs test scorers not to take off points for nonstandardized English features. If the test scorer is not well versed in language variation in general, is unfamiliar with the process of recognizing language variants, or is unfamiliar with features of the particular variety that a student speaks, it will be very difficult for that professional to make the needed accommodations in the assessment procedures.

One commonly used program to assess fluency on a range of reading-related tasks is DIBELS (Dynamic Indicators of Basic Early Literacy Skills). Used across the United States, DIBELS has become the primary assessment for K–3 students' reading skills (Shelton, Altwerger, & Jordan, 2009). DIBELS features a web-based database that allows schools and districts to enter their DIBELS data online and generate automated reports. Nevertheless, as Shelton and colleagues (2009) noted, skepticism about the wide-scale endorsement of DIBELS has mounted, particularly regarding the validity of DIBELS' measures of reading risk, as well as children's abilities to read and comprehend nontest reading material, otherwise known as authentic texts.

One concern surrounds DIBELS' instructions for assessing students with regard to language variation. For example, DIBELS provides the following instructions to examiners:

> #7, *Articulation and dialect*: The student is not penalized for imperfect pronunciation due to dialect, articulation, or second language interference. For example, if the student consistently says /th/ for /s/ and pronounces "thee" for "see" when naming the letter "C", he/she should be given credit for correct letter naming. This is a professional judgment and should be based on the student's responses and any prior knowledge of his/her speech patterns. (University of Oregon Center on Teaching and Learning, n.d., para. 18)

It is important that the instructions for DIBELS take into account language variation, yet examiners are still asked to notice relevant variants and use their "professional judgment" to assess them. No examiner could possibly be held responsible for identifying every variety of English and judging students' language features accordingly. Instead, specific guidelines must be established as to what features are likely to occur for a given population, and lists must be checked against the nonstandardized pronunciations of given students. For example, if, on a given test, young students are being assessed as to whether they produce the sound *arr* for the letter *r*, test scorers must be made aware that speakers of African American English often produce the *r* sound in a few different, regular ways. Similar precautions must also be taken when making important educational decisions, such as determining whether a student needs special education services (see Salvia, Ysseldyke, & Bolt, 2006).

Issues related to language variation may affect older test-taking students as well. For example, pronunciation differences may affect how Southern English–speaking students perceive less commonly used words that are often included on standardized tests. Words like *eminent* and *imminent* tend to give all students trouble, and students are generally told to remember differences in how the words are pronounced in order to help them tell the words apart. In Southern English, however, these words are pronounced exactly the same due to a vowel merger. Southern students are at a disadvantage when learning the differences between these words, as they cannot rely on pronunciation clues to help them.

The fact that pronunciation differences can hinder certain students when taking tests is particularly problematic considering that the advice "just sound it out" is often given to students struggling to find the correct answer. One popular SAT preparation manual advises that, first and foremost, students should read a given sentence or phrase to themselves and try to "hear" the error. Upon doing so, the manual explains, the mistake will often become immediately apparent. For linguistic reasons, however, speakers of nonstandardized varieties of English may hear, process, and interpret certain features of sentences in their mind's ear very differently. It is misleading and detrimental for students to be instructed to choose a correct answer based on listening and intuition alone, because test items frequently include nonstandardized language variants that are acceptable in students' home language varieties but count as mistakes in standardized English. Instead, educators can guide students to understand specific situations in which they may face certain linguistic challenges when answering common test questions.

Grammar

Grammatical differences may also affect nonstandardized English–speaking students' performance on standardized tests. One challenge is that test questions may ask students to answer *yes* or *no* to a series of statements. One commonly used standardized test includes the statement "You can eat an apple" and asks students to reply *yes* or *no*. The word *can* has two main meanings in everyday English, however: It can mean "to permit," or it can mean "to be physically able." Some test takers may take the first definition of *can* and interpret the question literally with respect to themselves, judging that at that moment they can*not* eat the apple because eating is not permitted during tests or in classrooms. Younger students, in particular, often produce such self-relative analysis. Younger students also may not know whether or not the abstract *you* that the test question is referring to is physically able to eat an apple. Moreover, Southern

English–speaking students, who often use and understand modal verbs in nonstandardized ways (e.g., in Southern English, the use of *might could* means something different than either the use of *might* or the use of *could*), may be at a disadvantage when it comes to answering test questions that rely on whether a student has a standardized comprehension of modal verbs.

Nonstandardized grammatical features, such as the absence of helping or linking forms of the verb *to be*, may yield special challenges for African American English–speaking students taking standardized tests. In one question, similar to those that routinely appear on standardized tests for young students, a student is presented with a picture of a bicycle. Underneath the picture, the text reads, "The bicycle _______ red," and students are asked to fill in the blank. In standardized English, the response that is considered correct is "The bicycle *is* red." In African American English, however, producing *is* is variable; it may or may not be produced. Therefore, the sentence "The bicycle red" is acceptable to African American English–speaking students as it stands, without having to fill in the blank at all. In this instance, it is difficult to discern what the test question is measuring, as it conflates an assessment of students' comprehension with their use of standardized English.

For many standardized test items, context clues are not available. Test questions may be asked in rapid-answer or fill-in-the-blank formats to assess word identification, word attack, and reading comprehension. When items are presented without context, learners who process language contextually are at a marked disadvantage. Questions that are asked in decontextualized formats may be especially difficult for students who are used to engaging in more topic-oriented and/or context-oriented interpretations, such as African American English–speaking students. Longer texts may also rely more on students possessing specific cultural knowledge, which may be disproportionately difficult for students whose cultural backgrounds are more distanced from those of test developers.

More advanced tests, including the SAT, also assess students' knowledge of specific standardized English features. The SAT writing section includes a 25-question section on "Improving Sentences" and an 18-question section on "Improving Sentence Errors." According to the College Board (2009), the "Improving Sentence Errors" section measures a test taker's ability to "recognize faults in usage [and] recognize effective sentences that follow the conventions of standard written English" (para. 1). Some of these test sentences that ask students to provide the correct answer in "standard written English" are disproportionately difficult for nonstandardized English–speaking students to answer.

The following example sentence is similar to questions found on the "Improving Sentence Errors" section of the SAT: "Ice cream sundaes with whipped cream and sprinkles, *although* delicious *if consumed* in moderation, *is sickening* if eaten *for dinner*." In this type of question, students determine whether one of the italicized portions of the sentence is an error or whether the sentence has no errors at all. The right answer, according to the test, is to mark *is sickening* as an error of subject–verb agreement (because *sundaes* is a plural subject and *is* is a singular verb). This type of question is much more difficult to answer, however, if a given test taker speaks a variety of English that allows regularization of the verb patterns for *is* and *are*. In many nonstandardized varieties, including Southern English and African American English, plural subjects like *sundaes* may take a singular verb. This process of verb regularization occurs particularly often when the plural subject ends in the *z* sound (as in *sundaes*), a sound that parallels the *z* sound in the word *is*.

The following sentence is also similar to questions found on the "Improving Sentence Errors" section of the SAT: "Katie *can't scarcely* stand to wear her *bookbag without* tightening the shoulder straps *underneath*." The right answer, according to the test, is to identify *can't scarcely* as an error, due to the use of the double negative. As Wolfram, Adger, and Christian (2007) noted, certain test questions may overpenalize Southern English–speaking students who use multiple negation. In the sample test question they give—"By the time Nick arrived at the campsite, the tents had been set up, the fire was lit, and there wasn't hardly anything to do except relax and enjoy the mountain air" (p. 122)—the right answer requires students to recognize that the presence of *wasn't* and *hardly* in the same sentence constitutes a nonstandardized pattern of negation. In Southern English, speakers commonly use negative adverbs like *barely, scarcely,* and *hardly* to add emphasis to their negative statements, and Southern students may conceive of these words as carrying an emphatic meaning, not a negative one. For Southern students, such test questions may appear to include no error, or the error may be harder to spot at first glance, causing students to require extra time to answer the question. Southern English–speaking students may need specific instruction as to the fact that negative adverbs are negative words, they may need to review the rules for marking negation in standardized English, and they may need to carefully review how questions containing multiple negation are asked on standardized tests such as the SAT.

Wolfram and colleagues (2007) also explained that many standardized test questions ask students to recognize other nonstandardized language variants and mark them as incorrect, as in such sentences as "Both novels deal with immigrants from Africa, who, overcoming obstacles, advance themself in America in spite of society's unjust treatment towards Black people" (p. 122). Students who speak nonstandardized varieties of English may need focused instruction to ensure they know that regularized possessive forms such as *themself, hisself,* and *theirselves* are considered to be errors in standardized English.

If nonstandardized English–speaking students are given accurate linguistic information about how their patterns of speech and writing may differ from the standardized English responses that are expected on standardized tests, and if students practice using this information, they will be in a much better position to do well on standardized tests. Students who speak nonstandardized varieties of English may need special assistance from educators to help them figure out the correct answers for questions that assess knowledge of the rules of standardized English, and students may also need help in practicing how to derive correct standardized English answers quickly on timed tests.

Pitch, Tone, Rhythm, and Volume

In addition to pronunciation and grammar, features that include pitch, tone, rhythm, volume, and speech rate are sometimes evaluated on standardized tests, often without acknowledging that these features are variable. Regarding standardized tests of reading assessment, Downhower (1997) discussed the fact that reading instructors are often asked to qualitatively evaluate students' intonation, mark students' fluency, and record their general level of engagement with the text. Fluency is generally assessed by a student's rate of speech when reading out loud, though there is no single target for what a student's rate of speech should be. Because of their tendency to speak a bit more slowly than other students, Southern English–speaking students in particular may be diagnosed as being less fluent in oral reading than they actually are.

Other common assessments, including assessments of kindergartners' literacy, ask test examiners to provide their own judgments of how fluent students sound. Without complete knowledge of the range of intonation, speech rate, and other features for all students, not just standardized English–speaking students, linguistic biases can emerge in scoring the tests. If intonation patterns that are characteristic of White women in American society are the de facto norm for assessing whether students sound fluent on tests of oral reading, some boys, particularly African American boys, may be overpenalized for failure to adhere to these conventions.

Common tests of nonverbal accuracy also measure how well test takers make judgments based on features such as tone of voice, pitch, volume, speech rate, and facial expressions. Collins and Nowicki (2001) demonstrated that African American test takers' performance on the Diagnostic Analysis of Nonverbal Accuracy (DANVA) is related to how well teachers perceive these students to be doing in school. The DANVA consists of 24 photographs of adult and child facial expressions that are meant to represent happiness, sadness, anger, and fear in both high and low intensities. The test takers are then supposed to link these emotions with different stimuli.

Collins and Nowicki (2001) studied 84 African American students' performance on the DANVA. These students were, on average, 10 years old and were enrolled in a private school. Collins and Nowicki found that these African American students had significantly different interpretations of the emotions depicted in the DANVA test questions, compared to their White peers in public schools, and the African American students did not as readily perceive the emotions that the White adult voices and faces were intended to carry. These African American students' performance on the DANVA was also significantly related to their general academic achievement. In light of Collins and Nowicki's findings, all students should be taught ways of recognizing specific standardized depictions of emotional expression if this type of material is to be included on standardized tests.

Other studies involving the DANVA have found gender effects with regard to interpreting emotions. Nowicki and Carton (1993) and Collins and Nowicki (2001) found that African American girls scored higher than African American boys on the section of the DANVA that asks students to evaluate emotions. The researchers hypothesized that girls who are better able to recognize adult emotions form stronger relationships with adults, including educators, and that these personal connections increase the students' rate of learning and promote their overall educational achievement. Based on their findings, Collins and Nowicki called for more research to be done on African American nonverbal and intonational cues so that the DANVA could be made culturally and linguistically sensitive.

Conversation

Some tests ask students to converse for a while with the examiner, who is always in a more powerful position than the student being evaluated. The hierarchical relationship between the test giver and the test taker may produce anxiety for the student. If the test giver is White and middle class and the student is from a different racial, ethnic, or economic background, the student may also feel wary and may, as a result, speak and act in a much more guarded way.

Many studies, including ones by Labov (1972), Morgan (2002), Craig and Washington (2006), and Green (2010), note the importance of understanding positions within hierarchies, since differences in the nature of relationships between African American students and the adults observing them can greatly influence students' responses in assessment situations. Common tactics when test givers are assessing language ability include visiting families' homes once a month and observing how parents and children interact. Families might be more guarded during outside observation, however—particularly when test givers are distanced from the students' and their families' social and cultural worlds—and therefore interact less naturally when they feel they are being watched closely and monitored. Among African Americans, this difference in how families act in the presence of outsiders is one of the lingering effects of segregation and historically disproportionate rates of intrusion of governmental agencies (e.g., police, social services) into the lives of African Americans.

Even in the best-case scenarios in which test takers are talking freely, cultural and linguistic differences may still emerge in ways that affect how language samples are judged and scored along standardized lines. When African American students are asked to provide speech samples and conversation samples, for example, the sentences and stories that they produce may be more elliptical (less linear) than those produced by standardized English–speaking students. For example, Feagans and Fendt (1991) gave African American children the task of orally retelling a story and found that children from low-income neighborhoods paraphrased the story less precisely than did their peers from middle-class neighborhoods. Feagans and Fendt did not interpret these results as indicating that lower-income African American students have weaker performance on story-retelling tasks. Instead, they contended that these students' story-retelling performances reflect the influences of an oral, African American cultural tradition that encourages creative verbal behaviors, such as elaboration, and supports different modes of storytelling, such as topic-associating narrative styles (discussed in Chapter 4).

STRATEGIES FOR EDUCATORS

Redd and Webb (2005) suggested that students practice their skills of paraphrasing and retelling stories from African American English into standardized English and vice versa. In this exercise, students listen to or read a story told in standardized English, and then, in cooperative learning groups, they retell the story in African American English. Using the same process in reverse, students listen to or read a story told in African American English and then, in groups, retell the story using standardized English.

In situations in which students are asked to converse with the examiner, differences in conversational norms and linguistic interpretations may lead examiners to misinterpret the attitudes and emotions of the test-taking students. Some African American English–speaking students may appear reticent, which examiners may interpret as sullenness or disengagement from the task at hand. Other African American English–speaking students may be perceived to be speaking more loudly and assertively, and examiners who expect test takers to display more modulated verbal behavior may interpret these students as acting aggressive or rebellious, or even as being angry. Indeed, Kochman (1981) found that Whites may perceive African Americans to be more intense in their expressions of emotion, particularly of anger, due to differences in cultural norms surrounding how to display and express emotion. Given these types of cultural differences, examiners must have knowledge of language variation among a given test-taking population, and instruments and situations for assessing students' language must be constructed in ways that take the norms of test takers' language varieties into account.

Vocabulary

Vocabulary is a critical part of demonstrating fluency in standardized English and succeeding on standardized tests. Many studies have suggested that students of lower socioeconomic status as well as Southern, Appalachian, and African American students come to school with a smaller standardized English vocabulary (though not necessarily a smaller *total* vocabulary) than middle-class children. Yet many test questions that attempt to gauge general aptitude are written based on the understanding that all students know certain standardized English vocabulary items. Such assumptions can lead the speech of nonstandardized English–speaking students to be misevaluated as developmentally delayed or less verbal than other students who are more familiar with standardized English vocabulary. To determine whether or not a test is appropriate for a given population requires taking into account the specific population on which a given test was normed and evaluating the suitability of the testing instrument based on the performance of the population being examined.

An important illustration of the need for linguistic awareness when assessing the vocabulary of nonstandardized English–speaking students can be seen in Hart and Risley (1995). Hart and Risley conducted a study in which they examined the speech of African American and White children of economically diverse backgrounds. The researchers and members of their research team spent 1 hour per month for 2 years in the homes of 42 families, African American and White, who varied in their economic status: professional, middle/working class, and low income. The researchers studied the amount and range of vocabulary items as well as the complexity of the sentences that the children in these 42 families used. During each hour of observation, Hart and Risley recorded every word that the parents and children uttered and then analyzed the patterns of verbal interaction. They used what they called "textbook definitions" to define and categorize the children's utterances and vocabulary, and they used "a standard dictionary to define words as nouns, verbs, modifiers, and functors" (p. 138).

Hart and Risley reported that differences surfaced along the lines of income level and race with respect to the amount and type of verbal interaction styles of the children and parents they studied. They concluded that the speech of the children from the economically disadvantaged and/or African American homes was more linguistically impoverished than the speech of the children from the economically advantaged and/or White homes. They suggested that these disparities pointed to different "conversational cultures" that children learn from birth, and they argued that the parents' limited verbal interactions with their children led directly to their children developing smaller vocabularies.

These conclusions overreach for several reasons. First, it is not surprising that variation is often found when researchers examine how different groups of speakers use language. Yet it is crucial to note that while standardized assessments of the vocabulary of lower-income and/or African American speakers may reveal differences in relation to their middle-class and/or White peers, sometimes this evidence is a by-product of the techniques for language measurement and analysis that were used. In other words, there are serious concerns with the ways that many language assessment situations, such as that of the Hart and Risley study, are carried out.

Language assessments, noted Wolfram (1998), are often "laden with values about language use, including the value of verbosity (the more you speak the better), . . . to say nothing of the asymmetrical power relations between the adult stranger and child" (p. 110). Children (and even adults) who may be talkative in relaxed, familiar settings may be reticent in testing situations or situations in which researchers are present and observing them. Examiners may therefore receive a false "appearance of nonverbalness," which may simply be "created by the artificial testing conditions under which language is sometimes collected for the purposes of assessment" (Wolfram, 1998, p. 111). The methodological circumstances of the Hart and Risley study therefore call into question the conclusions that were drawn. The fact that certain groups of parents and children were found to be quantitatively less verbose during observational situations is a limited and decontextualized finding. Results from counting a speaker's vocabulary size in observational settings must not be extrapolated to drawing generalized conclusions about that speaker's overall linguistic development, proficiency, and competence.

Moreover, it is incorrect to interpret evidence of language differences in ways that suggest that the language and culture of lower-socioeconomic-status and/or African American speakers—or even the speakers themselves—are inherently deficient. As Nunberg (2002) asserted with respect to Hart and Risley's study, "Whether you're disparaging the vocabularies of welfare mothers or the Cherokee, the claim always carries an unfortunate tone of condescension. It's easier to ignore people's voices when you've decided they couldn't possibly have one" (para. 8).

The methodological and interpretive limitations of studies such as Hart and Risley's (1995) notwithstanding, there is no question that a standardized English vocabulary is critical to students' success, both on standardized tests and in educational situations. The linguistic practices that are often used by middle-class, well-educated families are likely to be very similar to the language patterns that standardized tools are designed to assess (Dickinson, McCabe, Anastasopoulos, Peisner-Feinberg, & Poe, 2003). "Textbook definitions" that are often used in language assessment situations may therefore privilege the use of standardized language forms while failing to capture the nuances and complexities of nonstandardized communication patterns.

Because nonstandardized vocabulary items are frequently misunderstood, educators may want to pay particular attention to explicitly teaching a wide range of standardized vocabulary items to all students. Scarborough and colleagues (2003) found that the teaching of specific relational terms is essential for young students' comprehension of instructions on preliteracy assessments. Relational terms including *beginning, next,* and *next to last* are often employed on standardized tests of reading readiness, yet many kindergartners do not come to school with prior knowledge of these terms. As a result, students' aptitude may not be accurately assessed.

Hoover and colleagues (1995) also suggested that educators specifically introduce vocabulary items that may be unfamiliar due to students' cultural backgrounds as well as the region of the country that they come from. Words for housing and transportation, which often appear on nationally administered standardized tests, may be regionally variable. For example, students who grow up in dense urban areas may be more familiar with words such as *apartment, flat, co-op, walk-up,* and *brownstone,* whereas other students may be more familiar with words such as *condo, townhouse, farmhouse, split-level,* and *bungalow.* Students who grow up in

Philadelphia may refer to the sidewalk as *pavement,* but this vocabulary choice may not be considered correct on common standardized tests, on which *pavement* refers to the material (tar or cement) used to surface roads. In some parts of the United States, the words *train, subway,* and *metro* may be interchangeable, while in other regions each word may refer to a different mode of transportation.

Weather- and climate-related vocabulary items, which also frequently appear on standardized tests, may be variable as well, and some students may be unfamiliar with certain terms due to their regional background. For example, the word *toboggan* refers to a type of sled in the North but to a type of winter hat in the South. Boots that are worn in the rain may be called *galoshes, rain boots, rubber boots, rubbers, dickersons, overshoes, gumboots,* or *gumshoes,* depending on region.

Sometimes test questions are based on reading passages about experiences that students from certain regional areas may not have necessarily had. For example, Southern students may not go skiing as much as students from other parts of the United States; students who grow up in more tropical or arid climates in the South and West may only be familiar with two seasons; and students from urban areas may not go to the beach, pool, or shore—therefore related words that appear on standardized tests may be unfamiliar. Hernandez (2009) reported that some questions on New York State tests, including mathematical word problems, contained vocabulary items such as *stalk, swan, fox, milking,* and *plowing.* These words were highly challenging for students from New York City: The fact that they did not know the agricultural meanings of these terms affected their understanding of the test questions and their ability to answer them correctly.

Furthermore, African American students may be less familiar with vocabulary related to leisure travel, which may affect their performance on certain test items, such as reading a passage and answering questions about traveling to Europe. African Americans generally travel less than other racial and ethnic groups for many reasons, including the constraints that segregation historically placed on free movement; the economic situations of African Americans, who may have less expendable income for travel; and the fact that African Americans' safety and rights may not be guaranteed internationally as they are in domestic environments (Charity Hudley, 2009). Additional practice with vocabulary items and cultural concepts that are related to geographic places, travel, and leisure activities will help students understand such items on standardized tests.

When it comes to preparing students to succeed on high-stakes tests including the SAT, educators may adopt specific pedagogical strategies for increasing students' academic vocabularies. Having students make flashcards is not the only way for educators to increase students' academic vocabularies. Such exercises may be beneficial in some ways but may become monotonous or boring to students over time, and these techniques may have little value or relevance to students' lives outside of test preparation. Instead, students may be challenged to learn academic vocabulary items, including so-called SAT words, through more creative methods. At one tutoring center in Baltimore, Maryland, an African American male high school student named Dameon (a pseudonym) who was preparing for the SAT chose the following nine words from a list of SAT vocabulary items: *flippant, fiasco, fictitious, fledgling, fidelity, festive, frigid, frenzied,* and *furtive*. The tutor asked Dameon to look up each word in a dictionary and write a short definition for each. Then the tutor asked Dameon to practice the definitions either by making flashcards or by writing a poem or rap, in any writing style that felt comfortable to him, that incorporated each vocabulary word in a way that made sense and revealed the meaning of the word in context. Dameon wrote the following rap.

> Dese dudes out dere trippin, thinking I'm *flippant,*
> But I'm dead serious, and dey mad *fictitious.*
> Da boy got integrity and outstanding *fidelity,*
> Not a single felony, da feds can't mess wit me.
> Most rappers timid, my flow is so *frigid,*
> Datz intensively cold for you dudes dat's illiterate.
> U gotta commend me, cuz I leave the crowd *frenzied*
> While dese *furtive* rappers still tryna befriend me.
> Don't think I'm getting beat and not get avenging,
> Dese boys take a loss cuz dey all so *fledgling.*
> Da boy flow is heavy, can't weigh it in mass though,
> Dese dudes give up quick and dey suffer *fiasco.*
> I wasn't too *festive* when I settled for less
> Now that I'm on top I can settle as best.

As can be seen, Dameon produced a rap that is personally relevant, is coherent in its content, and accurately employs each of the nine vocabulary items. Context clues in the rap reveal that Dameon has a clear understanding of each word, and in one line he even included a definition for the listener (". . . my flow is so *frigid*/Datz intensively cold for you dudes dat's illiterate"). The rap contains numerous features of African American English, such as the absence of helping or linking forms of *be* ("Most rappers timid" for "Most rappers are timid") and the absence of possessive *-s* ("Da boy flow" for "Da boy's flow"). Dameon also represents some nonstandardized pronunciations with nonstandardized spellings (e.g., the use of *d* for the *th* sound, as in "Dese boys" for "These boys"), which lend a specific linguistic style to the rap.

From beginning to end, the assignment took Dameon only 45 minutes, and composing the rap itself took him less than half an hour. On most written assignments, Dameon tends to work much more slowly, but on this task, Dameon may have felt the freedom to compose his rap more quickly because he did not have to simultaneously focus on creative expression and on adhering to the spelling and grammar conventions of standardized English. Dameon enthusiastically agreed to have his rap published in this book, stating that he wanted other students to benefit from this technique for learning difficult vocabulary items. Weeks later, Dameon showed a continued facility with these words, employing them in other situations without having been prompted.

At the tutoring center, students are also engaged in writing poetry and fiction in ways that encourage them to develop their academic vocabulary while also writing in ways that feel comfortable to them. Similar techniques as well as follow-up exercises may be used: After students have written raps, poems, or fiction in a writing style that feels comfortable to them, educators may ask students to rewrite those texts in ways that adhere to the conventions of standardized English. These types of exercises help students develop their linguistic versatility. They may also help students improve their performance on standardized tests, such as the SAT. Hill (2009) found that when hip-hop was incorporated into a Philadelphia, Pennsylvania, high school literature classroom, student attendance and test performance rose. Other scholars (e.g., Alim, Ibrahim, & Pennycook, 2008; Ball & Lardner, 2005) have described the global impact of hip-hop culture in pedagogy as well.

STRATEGIES FOR EDUCATORS

Exercises in which students search for specific words in hip-hop song lyrics may help develop their vocabularies, thereby contributing to better performance on standardized tests. The hip-hop artist Mos Def has a large repertoire of songs that make use of many so-called SAT words. For example, lyrics to his song "Magnificent" (2004) included the words *congregate, efficient, envisioning, magnificent, omnipotent, recital,* and *relay,* and lyrics to his song "Love" (1999) included the words *evidence, infinite, landmark, portray, reverence, sentiment, tenderness,* and *temperament.* Students may examine the lyrics of these songs, identifying academic vocabulary items, drawing definitions for these words from context, and then looking up formal definitions.

Other rap and hip-hop artists whose song lyrics may be appropriate for students to analyze include Talib Kweli, Lauryn Hill, The Fugees, A Tribe Called Quest, and The Roots.

Baugh (1999) suggested a similar exercise called "Lyric Shuffle," in which students are asked to circle nonstandardized English features as well as standardized English features that appear in the lyrics of a song they like. Students then examine the various features that appear in the song, discuss their use and significance, and compare the linguistic features they found with those their classmates found in their songs.

Pictures and Images

In standardized English, multiple words may exist for the same item, and single words may have multiple meanings, yet creativity and knowing alternative ways of naming things are not skills that standardized tests typically assess. Reflecting this situation, Champion, Hyter, McCabe, and Bland-Stewart (2003) found that 11 words from the Peabody Picture Vocabulary Test–Third Edition had alternate meanings for African American children. For example, the researchers found that when the children taking the test heard the word *squash,* they often thought it meant "squash this," as in "to put an end to a particular activity." Because none of the choices of pictures provided on the test reflected this meaning, the children were frequently stymied. Champion and colleagues (2003) also found that the children taking the test interpreted the word *trunk* more often to refer to a person's derriere, and they tended to search for a picture of a human derriere instead of a picture of a tree trunk or a chest for holding items.

Picture vocabulary tests may also contain items that are unfamiliar to certain groups of test takers due to cultural, economic, or geographical differences (Garrett, 2009; Stockman, 2000; Washington & Craig, 1992). For example, Garrett (2009) found that African American children from Baltimore, Maryland, had particular difficulty interpreting pictures that were intended to represent the words *orchard, trail, hedge,* and *gravel.* These terms may be disproportionately difficult for students who live in urban areas to understand and recognize. Garrett (2009) also found that the children in her study had trouble interpreting a picture of melting ice and snow on a house as relating to the word *thaw.* Some students selected an incorrect word choice because they thought the image indicated that it was raining or that the house was leaking.

Other pictures and images that represent items that are seemingly general to American education may also be regionally specific. Pictures of a cherry tree or a magnolia tree, for example, may be harder to interpret for students who have grown up in urban areas or regions of the country where these trees are not commonly found. Students need practice becoming familiar with photographs and pictures of scenes of places that they may not have encountered in their daily lives, such as the beach, a desert, a city, ski slopes, and even traditional scenes of a Northeastern autumn or spring. Educators can introduce students from urban locales to suburban and rural imagery, students from rural and suburban backgrounds to urban imagery, and imagery of people who may not populate the local area to students who live in less diverse regions.

Some pictures and images used on standardized tests may also portray people in racially and ethnically biased ways. One item on a national test portrayed an Asian American family as being cross-eyed. Such blatant caricatures of racial and ethnic groups on standardized tests can fuel non-White students' anxiety and shame about racial stereotyping, stigma, and social expectations, thereby significantly affecting how they perform on standardized tests (Steele, 1992; Steele & Aronson, 1995).

Further Considerations

Some nonverbal assessment measures and tests do not require use of standardized English vocabulary items that many more privileged students receive at home or in preschool. As McCallum, Bracken, and Wasserman (2000) discussed, some nonverbal assessments provide a way around some of the linguistic biases found in verbal assessments. At the same time, many nonverbal norms are still based on specific cultural norms. Care must therefore always be taken when employing nonverbal tests and when assessing their reliability and validity.

As educators become increasingly knowledgeable about the cultural and social histories of standardized tests, they can better prepare students socially and academically for the process of test taking (Farr, Seloni, & Song, 2009). Educators can help students prepare for the demands of specific tests, while scholars can work to change unfair tests and testing situations. If practices are not changed, standardized tests will continue to overpenalize nonstandardized English–speaking students, as measurement techniques often require these students to understand and interpret a language and culture that is largely not their own. With the creation of more equitable tests, it becomes more possible to ensure that all students find educational success.

OTHER TYPES OF ASSESSMENT

In our educational system, assessing students' language is not limited to standardized testing situations. Language is discussed in many settings, including counseling, tutoring, and personal settings. Different cultural and linguistic norms are significant. Careful attention must therefore be paid to how evaluators decide which students sound engaged and eager, which students sound bored and noncompliant, and which students sound fluent—among many other emotions and behaviors. It is also critical to consider language variation when evaluating quiet or silent students as well as students who speak more loudly.

Counseling, tutoring, social work, language assessment, and many other types of professional situations often raise emotional and personal issues. As a result, the ways that students choose to communicate in these situations may be more or less expressive than the speech or writing that they produce in more impersonal, casual, or familiar situations. The ways in which students express themselves during face-to-face encounters with professional adults illuminate the fact that individuals express and represent their social and linguistic selves in myriad and complex ways (Brice Heath, 1983; Goffman, 1956). Understanding the linguistic nuances of counseling, tutoring, social work, speech and language therapy, and other situations may help professionals better relate to and work with all populations, not just students who come to these interactions speaking standardized English.

Speech/Language Therapy

According to Ball, Perkins, King, and Howard (2008), linguistic principles and methods can be usefully applied to the clinical study of language disabilities and assessment. Washington (1996) examined the factors that cause African American students to be referred for language services and placed into special education classes at a much higher rate than students from other racial or ethnic backgrounds. In the United States, African American students, both today and in the past, have been disproportionately placed in special education and are also more often diagnosed with speech/language problems, mental retardation, and emotional disturbance; these issues are all influenced by the assessment of language and communication (Cartledge & Dukes, 2008; Harry & Anderson, 1995; Keulen et al., 1998; Wyatt & Seymour, 1999).

Washington (1996) noted that the assessment of an individual student's language is a difficult task and that clinicians must obtain reliable samples from both the student and the student's target speech population to make an accurate assessment of aptitude and ability. Similarly, Wolfram (1994) suggested that African American English–speaking students' speech should be analyzed with an understanding of the norms of both standardized English and African American English. Stockman (1996) also noted that it is important to know what the general way of speaking is in the student's community; collaborations between linguists and speech/language pathologists may be necessary to determine this specific information.

Craig and Washington (2006) provided guidelines for how to more accurately assess nonstandardized English–speaking students in preschool through the fifth grade. For speech/language therapists who are concerned that test takers' use of African American English will negatively influence their test results, the Diagnostic Evaluation of Language Variation–Screening Test (DELV) (Seymour, Roeper, & de Villiers, 2003) was created. The DELV takes the developmental stages and linguistic differences of nonstandardized English–speaking students into account. It is both norm- and criterion-referenced, using representative samples of African American students from across the United States. The development of more linguistically informed tests, such as the DELV, is needed.

The Michigan Protocol for African American Language (Craig & Washington, 2006) measures both receptive and expressive language skills using informal and formal methods. The Protocol evaluates growth in a student's language skills based on the context of the individual student and his or her speech community. Each language skill is examined more than once, so that evaluations of students do not rest on single scores. Most importantly, the Protocol requires that clinicians be interculturally and linguistically competent, meaning that they must possess accurate and extensive knowledge about the language and culture of the population they are studying.

Washington (1996) noted that scoring adjustments can also be made for some tests. The Black English Sentence Scoring (BESS) procedure was designed to take into account language variations found in African American English, although the BESS is largely based on African American adult speech. Washington therefore advocated the creation of new tests. She pointed to the Minimal Competency Core (Stockman, 1996) as one example of a test that is more comprehensive and attuned to language variation found among African American students.

Counseling and Mental Health Services

Counselors are increasingly aware of the need to be attuned to the language backgrounds of their counselees in order to provide them with the best counseling services possible. Beaman (1994) maintained that it is necessary for mental health professionals to be cognizant of cultural biases against African American English in order to engage in effective therapeutic relationships with African Americans. Similarly, Chen-Hayes and colleagues (1999) contended that counselors and related practitioners must be attuned to the special needs of counselees who do not speak standardized English, as language is a critical cultural factor for individuals going through the counseling process. Chen-Hayes and colleagues pointed out myriad ways that standardized English–speaking counselees are privileged in counseling situations and stated that counselors must be careful not to perceive nonstandardized English–speaking clients as lacking in skills, intelligence, or ability because of variations in their language patterns. In order to better support clients from nonstandardized English–speaking backgrounds, Chen-Hayes and colleagues (1999) advocated that counselors work to understand the culturally situated nuances of linguistic behavior, as this information can help shed light on counselees' patterns of social interaction that might otherwise be unclear or confusing to counselors.

With information that paints a detailed picture of the nuances related to culture and communication, educators, clinicians, and practitioners will be better able to understand where and how linguistic and cultural differences occur in the populations they work with. The integration of multiple perspectives as academics and practitioners work together will best serve individuals from a variety of cultural, racial, ethnic, economic, regional, and educational backgrounds.

LANGUAGE-CENTERED ACTION PLANS FOR EDUCATORS

Resources and partnerships have been established between linguists and educators to address questions surrounding how best to educate multicultural and linguistically diverse student populations. Some of these initiatives have resulted in print-based materials, multimedia and online materials, educator-training workshops, and service-learning endeavors.

In workshops that we have held for K–12 educators, participants developed their linguistic awareness and learned about language variation in ways that were tailored to educational contexts (Charity Hudley & Mallinson, 2009). For example, as our workshop participants learned about academic registers, they explored their own ideas about the ways that educators typically communicate with their students. In another example, as our workshop participants learned that standardized tests must be carefully designed to avoid cultural and linguistic biases, they examined educational assessments relevant to their teaching, including developmental tests, writing tests, and end-of-year exams. As the educators gained knowledge about how cultural and linguistic differences surface and impact student achievement in educational situations, they felt better equipped to help students from all language backgrounds succeed in school.

Service-learning courses are another way that linguists have worked to integrate academic knowledge, research opportunities, and educational outreach, while involving students at their home academic institutions in the process (Wurr & Hellebrandt, 2007). Through service-learning projects, professors and their students have unique opportunities to share linguistic knowledge with educators and community members while learning from these partnerships as well. Service-learning initiatives are often carried out in diverse communities and are oriented toward social change.

Anne teaches an introductory undergraduate linguistics course that includes a service-learning component on African American English. During regular class meetings, she teaches about the linguistic, social, and educational contexts of African American English. Students then serve in the community for 4 hours per week by tutoring and mentoring African American English–speaking students in local schools. Christine also teaches linguistics courses that include service-learning components. Students learn about the language varieties spoken across the United States and work with educators in Baltimore schools to raise students' and educators' linguistic awareness and develop students' linguistic versatility.

Many practical challenges related to education can be addressed through service-learning endeavors that apply linguistic knowledge to address community and educational needs. Educators may therefore seek to develop partnerships between their schools and local colleges and universities in order to receive important language-related services.

CONCLUSION

Language and communication are central components of many of the serious challenges facing students in American schools. Educators with knowledge of language diversity are in a unique position to help all students succeed in school. As a longtime kindergarten teacher said during a workshop we led on language variation, "Language is the rope that all other educational issues are intertwined around" (Mallinson & Charity Hudley, 2010, p. 254). Given the centrality of language and communication, it is important to hold conversations about issues related to diversity in communication across the educational spectrum and in the education policy arena, for the benefit of all students and educators (Labov & Charity Hudley, 2010).

In this book as well as through our research and outreach, we have advocated a multicultural, multidisciplinary model of *linguistic awareness* that addresses contemporary, pressing educational challenges related to language and culture in the United States. As we work with educators across grade levels and academic subjects, we continue to strive to advance knowledge about and respect for linguistic and cultural diversity and to integrate information about language variation into classroom pedagogy and educational praxis. In so doing, we follow in the footsteps of those who have come before us in the multicultural education movement, working to ensure that all students in an increasingly diverse United States are educated in ways that value their voices and enable them to achieve to their highest potential.

Afterword

THIS BOOK REPRESENTS the critical next period in the evolution of sociolinguistic application. It certainly reflects the influences of the first generation of sociolinguists who attempted to apply the findings of their research to social and educational problems, but it also demonstrates the next wave of sociolinguistic application that integrates reflexivity, nuance, and realism into the mix. This is not simply another book in which sociolinguistic experts pontificate about what educators should do about the language varieties that children naturally and comfortably speak in their communities of origin—and bring to school with them.

One of the unique aspects of this book is its reflexivity, as the experiences of two outstanding next-wave researchers are interwoven into the theoretical, descriptive, and practical dimensions of language diversity. Linguists and educators have had more than their share of impersonal accounts of linguistic differences and education through external eyes. Instead, Charity Hudley and Mallinson tell us what they have experienced and how it has affected their application of knowledge. The authors fully understand that Southerners' views of language are critical to their culture and identity, and they empathize with that stance. Their firsthand accounts are reflected throughout this book in ways that allow readers not only to share their extensive, sophisticated knowledge of sociolinguistics and education but to participate in the personal stories of these researchers who have experienced what they talk about as well. Charity Hudley and Mallinson also demonstrate how they practice what they preach through engaged scholarship, service-learning, and other community- and school-based programs, which sets this book apart from other collections about education and language variation.

Another dimension distinguishes the perspective of this book: the heightened sensitivity to the complexity and nuances of standardized English. While no one can question the authors' commitment to the fundamental premises of linguistic equality for all language varieties, Charity

Hudley and Mallinson also understand the significant choices involved in selecting language varieties and registers, including the standardized English that we use in our lectures and in our writing—including this epilogue. The authors pay attention to the value and roles of standardized English in the diverse circumstances of our lives, just as they do with non-standardized varieties. They give each variety a nuanced consideration that is realistically appropriate for the lives of students as well as adults.

Finally, there is a sensibility and wisdom in how Charity Hudley and Mallinson frame language within a broader context of social and educational reality. Their discussion of assessment in the final chapter identifies the critical role of language differences in the interpretation of test data. At the same time, the authors position this linguistic information alongside the many factors that affect assessment, including early socialization, self-fulfilling prophecies, health, and lifestyle. Language differences and sociolinguistic awareness therefore are established as being one important aspect of complex and multifaceted social, cultural, and educational challenges.

This is a landmark book in the consideration of language differences and education in the American South and throughout the United States. It guides linguists and educators as we all work to apply our knowledge on behalf of those for whom it matters most: students.

—Walt Wolfram
William C. Friday Distinguished Professor
of English Linguistics, North Carolina State University

References

Abedi, J., & Lord, C. (2001). The language factor in mathematics tests. *Applied Measurement in Education, 14*(3), 219–234.

Alim, H. S., Ibrahim, A., & Pennycook, A. (2008). *Global linguistic flows: Hip hop cultures, youth identities, and the politics of language*. New York: Routledge.

Alon, S., & Tienda, M. (2007). Diversity, opportunity, and the shifting meritocracy in higher education. *American Sociological Review, 72*(4), 487–511.

Alvarez, L., & Kolker, A. (Producers and Directors). (1988). *American tongues* [Film]. New York: PBS/Center for New American Media.

Anderson, J. D. (1988). *The education of Blacks in the South, 1860–1935*. Chapel Hill: University of North Carolina Press.

Andrews, L. (2006). *Language exploration and awareness: A resource book for teachers* (3rd ed.). Philadelphia: Erlbaum.

Applebee, A. N., & Langer, J. A. (2009). What is happening in the teaching of writing? *English Journal, 98*(5), 18–28.

ARC (Appalachian Regional Commission) homepage. (n.d.). Retrieved July 29, 2009, from http://www.arc.gov/index.jsp

Atchison, D. (Director). (2006). *Akeelah and the bee* [Film]. Los Angeles: Lions Gate Films.

Atkins v. Virginia, 536 U.S. 304 (2002).

Baldwin, J. (1985). If Black English isn't a language, then tell me, what is? In *The price of the ticket: Collected nonfiction, 1948–1985* (pp. 649–652). New York: St. Martin's/Marek.

Ball, A. F. (2000). Empowering pedagogies that enhance the learning of multicultural students. *Teachers College Record, 102*(6), 1006–1034.

Ball, A. F., & Lardner, T. (2005). *African American literacies unleashed: Vernacular English and the composition classroom*. Carbondale: Southern Illinois University Press.

Ball, M. J., Perkins, M. R., King, N., & Howard, S. (Eds.). (2008). *The handbook of clinical linguistics*. Malden, MA: Blackwell.

Banks, J. A., & Banks, C. A. M. (Eds.). (2004). *Handbook of research on multicultural education* (2nd ed.). San Francisco: Jossey-Bass.

Baugh, J. (1999). *Out of the mouths of slaves: African American language and educational malpractice.* Austin: University of Texas Press.

Baugh, J. (2000). *Beyond Ebonics: Linguistic pride and racial prejudice.* New York: Oxford University Press.

Beaman, D. (1994). Black English and the therapeutic relationship. *Journal of Mental Health Counseling, 16*(3), 379–386.

Bender, M. C. (2002). *Signs of Cherokee culture: Sequoyah's syllabary in Eastern Cherokee life.* Chapel Hill: University of North Carolina Press.

Bertrand, M., & Mullainathan, S. (2003). Enjoying the quiet life? Corporate governance and managerial preferences. *Journal of Political Economy, 111*(5), 1043–1075.

Birch, B. M. (2005). *Learning and teaching English grammar, K–12.* Upper Saddle River, NJ: Pearson/Merrill/Prentice Hall.

Blake, R., Fix, S., & Shousterman, C. (2009, January). Vowel centralization before /r/ in two AAE dialects. Paper presented at the Linguistic Society of America, San Francisco.

Blankenship, B. (1998). *1924 Baker Roll: The final roll of the Eastern band of Cherokee Indians of North Carolina.* Cherokee, NC: Cherokee Roots.

Bonfiglio, T. P. (2002). *Race and the rise of standard American.* Berlin: Mouton de Gruyter.

Brice Heath, S. (1983). *Ways with words: Language, life and work in communities and classrooms.* Cambridge, UK: Cambridge University Press.

Brizee, H. A. (2007, September 28). Paramedic method: A lesson in writing concisely. *The OWL at Purdue.* Retrieved August 24, 2009, from http://owl.english.purdue.edu/owl/resource/635/01/

Bullock, L. (2006, August 20). Testers posing as Katrina survivors encounter "linguistic profiling." *New America Media.* Retrieved November 3, 2009, from http://news.newamericamedia.org/news/view_article.html?article_id=88d97b82640f6ba16f5e07d9d695a1b3

Carroll, J. A., Wilson, E., & Forlini, G. (2001). *Writing and grammar: Communication in action: Platinum level* (annotated teacher's edition). Upper Saddle River, NJ: Prentice Hall.

Carter, P. L. (2007). *Keepin' it real: School success beyond black and white.* New York: Oxford University Press.

Cartledge, G., & Dukes, C. (2008). Disproportionality of African American children in special education: Definition and dimensions. In L. C. Tillman (Ed.), *The SAGE handbook of African American education* (pp. 383–398). Thousand Oaks, CA: Sage Publications.

Cazden, C. B. (1990). Differential treatment in New Zealand: Reflections on research in minority education. *Teaching and Teacher Education, 6*(4), 291–303.

Cazden, C. B. (2001). *Classroom discourse: The language of teaching and learning* (2nd ed.). Portsmouth, NH: Heinemann.

Champion, T. B., Hyter, Y. D., McCabe, A., & Bland-Stewart, L. M. (2003). "A matter of vocabulary": Performances of low-income African American Head Start children on the Peabody Picture Vocabulary Test–III. *Communication Disorders Quarterly, 24*(3), 121–127.

Charity, A. H. (2005). *Dialect variation in school settings among African-American children of low-socioeconomic status.* Unpublished doctoral dissertation, University of Pennsylvania, Philadelphia.

Charity, A. H. (2007). Regional differences in low SES African-American children's speech in the school setting. *Language Variation and Change, 19*(3), 281–293.

Charity Hudley, A. H. (2008). African American English. In D. H. A. Neville, D. B. M. Tynes, & D. S. O. Utsey (Eds.), *Handbook of African American psychology* (pp. 199–210). Thousand Oaks, CA: Sage Publications.

Charity, A. H. (2008a). African-American English: An overview. *Perspectives on Communication Disorders and Sciences in Culturally and Linguistically Diverse Populations, 15*(2), 33–42.

Charity, A. H. (2008b). Linguists as agents for social change. *Language and Linguistics Compass, 2*, 923–939.

Charity Hudley, A. H. (2009). Standardized assessment of African-American children: A sociolinguistic perspective. In M. Farr, L. Seloni, & J. Song (Eds.), *Ethnolinguistic diversity and education: Language, literacy and culture* (pp. 167–193). London: Routledge.

Charity Hudley, A. H., & Mallinson, C. (2009). *Language variation in the classroom: An educator's toolkit* (Summer Workshop Series). Richmond, VA: Virginia Commonwealth University.

Charles, C. Z., Roscigno, V. J., & Torres, K. C. (2007). Racial inequality and college attendance: The mediating role of parental investments. *Social Science Research, 36*(1), 329–352.

Chaucer, G. (2005). *The Canterbury tales (original-spelling Middle English edition).* New York: Penguin Classics.

Chaucer, G. (2008). *The Canterbury tales* (D. S. Wright, Trans.). New York: Oxford University Press.

Chen-Hayes, S. F., Chen, M., & Athar, N. (1999). Challenging linguicism: Action strategies for counselors and client-colleagues. In J. Lewis & L. Bradley (Eds.), *Advocacy in counseling: Counselors, clients, & community* (pp. 21–31). Greensboro, NC: ERIC Counseling and Student Services Clearinghouse.

Clifton, L. (1975). *My brother fine with me.* New York: Holt, Rinehart and Winston.

Coates, T. (2009, January 7). Added bonus: Irregardless of what you think, "conversate" is a word. *The Atlantic Monthly.* Retrieved August 31, 2009, from http://ta-nehisicoates.theatlantic.com/archives/2009/01/ask_the_expert_is_conversate_a_word.php

Cole, B. (1995). College admissions and coaching. In A. G. Hilliard (Ed.), *Testing African American students* (2nd ed., pp. 97–110). Chicago: Third World Press.

Cole, J., Thomas, E., Britt, E., & Coggshall, E. (2005, October). *Intonational distinctiveness of African American English.* Paper presented at the New Ways of Analyzing Variation 34, New York.

College Board. (2009). Identifying sentence errors. Retrieved August 1, 2009, from http://www.collegeboard.com/student/testing/sat/prep_one/sent_errors/pracStart.html

Collins, M., & Nowicki, S. (2001). African American children's ability to identify emotion in facial expressions and tones of voice of European Americans. *Journal of Genetic Psychology, 162*(3), 334–336.

Corcoran, S. P., Evans, W. N., & Schwab, R. M. (2004). Women, the labor market, and the declining relative quality of teachers. *Journal of Policy Analysis and Management, 23*(3), 449–470.

Craig, H. K., Thompson, C. A., Washington, J. A., & Potter, S. L. (2003). Phonological features of child African American English. *Journal of Speech, Language, and Hearing Research, 46*(3), 623–635.

Craig, H. K., & Washington, J. A. (2002). Oral language expectations for African American preschoolers and kindergartners. *American Journal of Speech-Language Pathology, 11*(1), 59–70.

Craig, H. K., & Washington, J. A. (2004). Grade-related changes in the production of African American English. *Journal of Speech, Language, and Hearing Research, 47*(2), 450–463.

Craig, H. K., & Washington, J. A. (2006). *Malik goes to school: Examining the language skills of African American students from preschool to fifth grade*. Mahwah, NJ: Erlbaum.

Dandy, E. B. (1991). *Black communications: Breaking down the barriers*. Chicago: African American Images.

Darling-Hammond, L. (2010). *The flat world and education: How America's commitment to equity will determine our future*. New York: Teachers College Press.

Day-Vines, N. L., & Day-Hairston, B. O. (2005). Culturally congruent strategies for addressing the behavioral needs of urban, African American male adolescents. *Professional School Counseling, 8*(3), 236–244.

Delpit, L. D., & Dowdy, J. K. (Eds.). (2008). *The skin that we speak: Thoughts on language and culture in the classroom*. New York: New Press.

DeShano da Silva, C., Huguley, J. P., Kakli, Z., & Rao, R. (Eds.). (2007). *The opportunity gap: Achievement and inequality in education*. Cambridge, MA: Harvard Educational Publishing Group.

DeYoung, A. J. (1995). Constructing and staffing the cultural bridge: The school as change agent in rural Appalachia. *Anthropology & Education Quarterly, 26*(2), 168–192.

Dickinson, D. K., Darrow, C. L., & Tinubu, T. (2008). Patterns of teacher-child conversations in Head Start classrooms: Implications for an empirically grounded approach to professional development. *Early Education and Development, 19*(3), 396–429.

Dickinson, D. K., McCabe, A., Anastasopoulos, L., Peisner-Feinberg, E., & Poe, M. D. (2003). The comprehensive language approach to early literacy: The interrelationships among vocabulary, phonological sensitivity, and print knowledge among preschool-aged children. *Journal of Educational Psychology, 95*(3), 464–481.

Dickmann, M. H., Stanford-Blair, N., & Rosati-Bojar, A. (2004). *Leading with the brain in mind: 101 brain-compatible practices for leaders*. Thousand Oaks, CA: Corwin.

Dillon, S. (2009, October 14). Sluggish results seen in math scores. *New York Times*.

Retrieved October 29, 2009, from http://www.nytimes.com/2009/10/15/education/15math.html?_r=1

Downhower, S. (1997). Effects of repeated readings techniques on second-grade transitional readers' fluency and comprehension. *Reading Research Quarterly, 22,* 389–406.

Du Bois, W. E. B. (1903). *The souls of Black folk.* Chicago: A.C. McClurg & Co.

Dunn, P. A., & Lindblom, K. (2003). Why revitalize grammar? *The English Journal, 92*(3), 43–50.

Dyer, J. (Ed.). (1998). *Bloodroot: Reflections on place by Appalachian women writers.* Lexington: University of Kentucky Press.

Eckert, P. (1989). *Jocks and burnouts: Social categories and identity in the high school.* New York: Teachers College Press.

Eckert, P., & McConnell-Ginet, S. (2003). *Language and gender.* Cambridge, UK: Cambridge University Press.

Erickson, F. (2007). Culture in society and in educational practices. In J. Banks & C. Banks (Eds.), *Multicultural education: Issues and perspectives* (7th ed., pp. 33–58). New York: John Wiley & Sons.

Evans-Winters, V. E. (2005). *Teaching Black girls: Resiliency in urban classrooms.* New York: Peter Lang.

Fama, M. E. (2007). *Talking Southern in Virginia: Investigating the presence of /ay/ monophthongization.* Unpublished senior thesis, College of William & Mary, Williamsburg, VA.

Farr, M., Seloni, L., & Song, J. (Eds.). (2009). *Ethnolinguistic diversity and education: Language, literacy, and culture.* New York: Routledge.

Feagans, L., & Fendt, K. (1991). The effects of intervention and social class on children's answers to concrete and abstract questions. *Journal of Applied Developmental Psychology, 12,* 115–130.

Feagin, J. R., Vera, H., & Imani, N. (1996). *The agony of education: Black students at White colleges and universities.* New York: Routledge.

Feldman, M. (Director). (1980). *In God we tru$t* [Film]. Los Angeles: Universal Pictures.

Ferguson, A. A. (2001). *Bad boys: Public schools in the making of Black masculinity.* Ann Arbor: University of Michigan Press.

Fischer, C. S., Hout, M., Jankowski, M. S., Lucas, S. R., Swidler, A., & Voss, K. (1996). *Inequality by design: Cracking the bell curve myth.* Princeton, NJ: Princeton University Press.

Fischer, J. L. (1958). Social influences on the choice of a linguistic variant. *Word, 14,* 47–56.

Fleming, V. (Director). (1939). *Gone with the wind* [Film]. Agoura Hills, CA: Metro-Goldwyn-Mayer.

Fogel, H., & Ehri, L. C. (2000). Teaching elementary students who speak Black English Vernacular to write in Standard English: Effects of dialect transformation practice. *Contemporary Educational Psychology, 25*(2), 212–235.

Fordham, S. (1993). "Those loud Black girls": (Black) women, silence, and gender "passing" in the academy. *Anthropology & Education Quarterly, 24*(1), 3–32.

Fordham, S. (1996). *Blacked out: Dilemmas of race, identity, and success at Capital High*. Chicago: University of Chicago Press.

Fordham, S., & Ogbu, J. U. (1986). Black students' school success: Coping with the "burden of 'acting White'." *The Urban Review, 18*(3), 176–206.

Foster, M. (1989). "It's cookin' now": A performance analysis of the speech events of a Black teacher in an urban community college. *Language in Society, 18*(1), 1–29.

Frankenberg, E., & Orfield, G. (2006). New Harvard research on the segregation of American teachers. Retrieved July 29, 2009, from http://www.civilrightsproject.ucla.edu/news/pressreleases/segregation_american_teachers.php

Garrett, A. (2009). *The role of picture perception in children's performance on a picture vocabulary test*. Unpublished doctoral dissertation, UMBC, Baltimore.

Gay, G. (1994). A *synthesis of scholarship in multicultural education* (Urban Education Monograph Series). Seattle: NCREL Urban Education Program.

Gershenberg, I. (1970). Southern values and public education: A revision. *History of Education Quarterly, 10*(4), 413–422.

Gilyard, K. (1996). *Let's flip the script: An African American discourse on language, literature, and learning*. Detroit: Wayne State University Press.

Godley, A. J., Sweetland, J., Wheeler, R. S., Minnici, A., & Carpenter, B. D. (2006). Preparing teachers for dialectally diverse classrooms. *Educational Researcher, 35*(8), 30–37.

Goffman, E. (1956). The nature of deference and demeanor. *American Anthropologist, 58*(3), 473–502.

Goodman, K. S., & Buck, C. (1973). Dialect barriers to reading comprehension revisited. *The Reading Teacher, 27*, 6–12.

Goodman, Y. M. (2003). *Valuing language study: Inquiry into language for elementary and middle schools*. Urbana, IL: National Council of Teachers of English.

Grant, L. (2004). Everyday schooling and the elaboration of race-gender stratification. In J. Ballantine & J. Spade (Eds.), *Schools and society* (2nd ed., pp. 296–307). Belmont, CA: Wadsworth.

Green, L. J. (2002). *African American English: A linguistic introduction*. Cambridge, UK: Cambridge University Press.

Green, L. J. (2010). *Language and the African American child*. Cambridge, UK: Cambridge University Press.

Greenwald, M. (Director). (2000). *Songcatcher* [Film]. Ashville, NC: Lions Gate Films.

Grogger, J. (2008, June). *Speech patterns and racial wage inequality* (Harris School Working Paper Series 08.13). Harris School of Public Policy, University of Chicago.

Gumperz, J., & Hernández-Chavez, E. (1972). Bilingualism, bidialectalism, and classroom interaction. In C. B. Cazden, V. P. John, & D. H. Hymes (Eds.), *Functions of language in the classroom* (pp. 84–108). New York: Teachers College Press.

Guy, G. (1980). Variation in the group and in the individual: The case of final stop deletion. In W. Labov (Ed.), *Locating language in time and space* (pp. 1–36). New York: Academic Press.

Hacker, D. (2008). *A pocket style manual* (5th ed.). Boston: Bedford/St. Martin's.

Hacker, D. (n.d.). Who versus whom. *A Pocket Style Manual.* Companion Website. Retrieved July 30, 2009, from http://bcs.bedfordstmartins.com/Pocket5e/player/pages/Frameset.aspx?edition=Pocket5e&sTabNo=9&sViewAs=S&sLMS=&subpageid=whowhom

Hansberry, L. (1959). *A raisin in the sun.* New York: Modern Library.

Hanson, S. L. (2009). *Swimming against the tide: African American girls and science education.* Philadelphia: Temple University Press.

Harper, D. (2003). Slavery in the North. Retrieved October 29, 2009, from http://www.slavenorth.com/index.html

Harry, B., & Anderson, M. G. (1995). The disproportional placement of African American males in special education programs. *Journal of Negro Education, 63*(4), 602–619.

Hart, B., & Risley, T. R. (1995). *Meaningful differences in the everyday experience of young American children.* Baltimore, MD: Brookes.

Hartman, L. (2000). Hollerin'. *All things considered* (National public radio). Retrieved August 24, 2009, from http://www.npr.org/templates/story/story.php?storyId=1076273

Hernandez, J. C. (2009, October 20). A moo-moo here, and better test scores later. *New York Times.* Retrieved October 29, 2009, from http://www.nytimes.com/2009/10/20/education/20farms.html

Higgs, R., Manning, A., & Miller, J. W. (1995). *Appalachian inside out: Culture and custom.* Knoxville: University of Tennessee Press.

Hill, M. L. (2009). *Beats, rhymes, and classroom life: Hip-hop pedagogy and the politics of identity.* New York: Teachers College Press.

hooks, b. (1999). *Talking back: Thinking feminist, thinking black.* Boston: South End Press.

Hoover, M., Politzer, R., & Taylor, O. (1995). Bias in reading tests for Black language speakers: A sociolinguistic perspective. In A. G. Hilliard (Ed.), *Testing African American students* (2nd ed., pp. 51–68). Chicago: Third World Press.

Howard, G. R. (2006). *We can't teach what we don't know: White teachers, multiracial schools* (2nd ed.). New York: Teachers College Press.

Hudson, B. H. (1993). Sociolinguistic analysis of dialogues and first-person narratives in fiction. In A. W. Glowka & D. M. Lance (Eds.), *Language variation in North American English: Research and teaching* (pp. 28–36). New York: Modern Language Association of America.

Hunt, L. L., Hunt, M. O., & Falk, W. W. (2008). Who is headed South? US migration trends in black and white, 1970–2000. *Social Forces, 87*(1), 95–119.

Hutcheson, N. (Director). (2004). *Mountain talk: Language and life in Southern Appalachia* [Film]. Raleigh, NC: North Carolina Language and Life Project.

Hutcheson, N. (Director). (2005). *Voices of North Carolina: Language, dialect, and identity in the Tarheel state* [Film]. Raleigh, NC: North Carolina Language and Life Project.

Johnson, R. (2008, November 8). Sir and ma'am: A Southern thing? *Aiken Standard.* Retrieved October 29, 2009, from http://www.aikenstandard.com/Local/1030Sir

Jonsson, P. (2007). The Southern drawl: Is it spreading? *ABC News*. Retrieved July 29, 2009, from http://abcnews.go.com/print?id=3637113

Jun, S., & Foreman, C. (1996, December). Boundary tones and focus realization in African-American intonation. Paper presented at the third joint meeting of the Acoustical Society of America and the Acoustical Society of Japan, Honolulu.

Kainz, K., & Vernon-Feagans, L. (2007). The ecology of early reading development for children in poverty. *Elementary School Journal, 107*(5), 407–427.

Keulen, J. E. v., Weddington, G. T., & DeBose, C. E. (1998). *Speech, language, learning, and the African American child*. Boston: Allyn & Bacon.

Koch, L. M., Gross, A. M., & Kolts, R. (2001). Attitudes toward Black English and code switching. *Journal of Black psychology, 27*(1), 29–42.

Kochhar, R., Suro, R., & Tafoya, S. (2005). The new Latino South: The context and consequences of rapid population growth. Retrieved July 29, 2009, from http://pewhispanic.org/reports/report.php?ReportID=50

Kochman, T. (1981). *Black and White styles in conflict*. Chicago: University of Chicago Press.

Koops, C. (2006, November). *"I tell you what" between discourse and regional English*. Poster presented at the New Ways of Analyzing Variation 35, Columbus, OH.

Kozol, J. (2005). *The shame of the nation: The restoration of apartheid schooling in America*. New York: Crown.

Labov, W. (1972). *Language in the inner city: Studies in the Black English Vernacular*. Philadelphia: University of Pennsylvania Press.

Labov, W. (1995). Can reading failure be reversed? A linguistic approach to the question. In V. L. Gadsden & D. A. Wagner (Eds.), *Literacy among African-American youth: Issues in learning, teaching, and schooling* (pp. 39–68). Creskill, NJ: Hampton Press.

Labov, W. (2001). *Principles of linguistic change*: *Vol. 2. Social factors*. Malden, MA: Blackwell.

Labov, W. (2006). Spotlight on reading. Retrieved November 3, 2009, from http://www.ling.upenn.edu/~wlabov/Spotlight.pdf

Labov, W. (2008). Unendangered dialects, endangered people. In K. King, N. Schilling-Estes, L. W. Fogle, J. J. Lou, & B. Soukup (Eds.), *Sustaining linguistic diversity: Endangered and minority languages and language varieties* (pp. 219–238). Washington, DC: Georgetown University Press.

Labov, W., Ash, S., & Boberg, C. (2006). *The Atlas of North American English*. Berlin: Mouton de Gruyter.

Labov, W., & Baker, B. (2003). What is a reading error? Retrieved August 1, 2009, from http://www.ling.upenn.edu/%7Ewlabov/Papers/WRE.html

Labov, W., & Charity Hudley, A. H. (2010). *Symbolic and structural effects of dialects and immigrant minority languages in explaining achievement gaps*. Menlo Park, CA: National Research Council/National Academy of Sciences' Committee on Language and Education.

Labov, W., Soto-Hinman, I., Dickson, S. V., Charity Hudley, A. H., & Thorsnes,

B. (2010). *Portals to reading: Intensive intervention*. Boston: Houghton Mifflin Harcourt.

Ladson-Billings, G. (2009). *The dreamkeepers: Successful teachers of African American children* (2nd ed.). San Francisco: Jossey-Bass.

Lager, C. A. (2006). Types of mathematics-language reading interactions that unnecessarily hinder algebra learning and assessment. *Reading Psychology, 27*(2–3), 165–204.

Langer, J. (2002). *Effective literacy instruction: Building successful reading and writing programs*. Urbana, IL: National Council of Teachers of English.

Larry P. v. Riles, 495 F. Supp. 926 (N.D. Cal. 1979).

Larry P. v. Riles, 793 F.2d 969 (9th Cir. 1984).

Lazerson, M. (1983). The origins of special education. In J. Chambers & W. Hartman (Eds.), *Special education policies: Their history, implementation, and finance* (pp. 3–47). Philadelphia: Temple University Press.

Lee, C. D. (2006). Every good-bye ain't gone: Analyzing the cultural underpinnings of classroom talk. *International Journal of Qualitative Studies in Education, 19*(3), 305–327.

Lee, C. D. (2007). *Culture, literacy, and learning: Taking bloom in the midst of the whirlwind*. New York: Teachers College Press.

Lemann, N. (1995, September). The great sorting [Electronic version]. *The Atlantic Monthly, 276*(3), 84–100. Retrieved May 30, 2010, from http://www.theatlantic.com/past/docs/issues/95sep/ets/grtsort2.htm

Lemann, N. (1999). *The big test: The secret history of the American meritocracy*. New York: Farrar, Straus & Giroux.

Lester, J. (1987). *The tales of Uncle Remus: The adventures of Brer Rabbit*. New York: Dial Books.

Lippi-Green, R. (1997). *English with an accent: Language, ideology, and discrimination in the United States*. London: Routledge.

Lyman, F. (1981). The responsive classroom discussion: The inclusion of all students. In A. Anderson (Ed.), *Mainstreaming digest* (pp. 109–113). College Park, MD: University of Maryland Press.

Lynch, J. (2009). The lexicographer's dilemma: The evolution of "proper" English, from Shakespeare to *South park*. New York: Walker.

MacNeil, R., & Cran, W. (2005). *Do you speak American?: A companion to the PBS television series*. New York: Nan A. Talese.

Major, C. (Ed.). (1994). *Juba to jive: The dictionary of African-American slang*. New York: Penguin.

Mallinson, C., & Charity Hudley, A. H. (2010). Communicating about communication: Multidisciplinary approaches to educating educators about language variation. *Language and Linguistics Compass, 4*, 245–257.

Mallinson, C., & Kendall, T. (2009). "The way I can speak for myself": The social and linguistic context of counseling interviews with African American adolescent girls in Washington, DC. In S. Lanehart (Ed.), *African American women's language: discourse, education, and identity* (pp. 110–126). Newcastle upon Tyne, UK: Cambridge Scholars Publishing.

Marin, V. (2002, May 20). Nickname creation in the South: Why Southern grandparents have such varied monikers. Retrieved October 29, 2009, from http://www.suite101.com/article.cfm/folklore/91852

Martin, J. R. (1983). The development of register. In J. Fine & R. Freedle (Eds.), *Developmental issues in discourse* (pp. 1–40). Norwood, NJ: Ablex.

Massey, D. S., & Denton, N. (1993). *American apartheid: Segregation and the making of the underclass*. Cambridge, MA: Harvard University Press.

Massey, D. S., & Lundy, G. (2001). Use of Black English and racial discrimination in urban housing markets: New methods and findings. *Urban Affairs Review, 36*(4), 452–469.

McCallum, R. S., Bracken, B., & Wasserman, J. (2000). *Essentials of nonverbal assessment*. New York: John Wiley & Sons.

McConchie, A. (n.d.). The pop vs. soda page. *The great pop vs. soda controversy*. Retrieved July 30, 2009, from http://popvssoda.com:2998/

McIntosh, P. (1988). White privilege: Unpacking the invisible knapsack. In *White privilege and male privilege: A personal account of coming to see correspondences through work in women's studies*. Wellesley, MA: Wellesley College Center for Research on Women.

McKissack, P. (1986). *Flossie and the fox*. New York: Dial.

McNeely, R. L., & Badami, M. K. (1984). Interracial communication in school social work. *Social Work, 29*(1), 22–26.

McWhiney, G. (1988). *Cracker culture: Celtic ways in the old South*. Tuscaloosa: University of Alabama Press.

Mehan, H. (1979). *Learning lessons: Social organization in the classroom*. Cambridge, MA: Harvard University Press.

Michaels, S. (1981). "Sharing time": Children's narrative styles and differential access to literacy. *Language in Society, 10*(3), 423–442.

Michaels, S., & Cazden, C. B. (1986). Teacher/child collaboration as oral preparation for literacy. In B. Schieffelin & P. Gilmore (Eds.), *The acquisition of literacy: Ethnographic perspectives* (pp. 132–154). Norwood, NJ: Ablex.

Michaels, S., O'Connor, C., & Resnick, L. B. (2008). Deliberative discourse idealized and realized: Accountable talk in the classroom and in civic life. *Studies in Philosophy and Education, 27*(4), 283–297.

Mishoe, M., & Montgomery, M. (1994). The pragmatics of multiple modal variation in North and South Carolina. *American Speech, 69*(1), 3–29.

Montgomery, M. (1992). The etymology of y'all. In J. H. Hall, N. Doane, & D. Ringler (Eds.), *Old English and new: Studies in language and linguistics in honor of Frederic G. Cassidy* (pp. 356–369). New York: Garland.

Montgomery, M. (1999). In the Appalachians they speak like Shakespeare. In L. Bauer & P. Trudgill (Eds.), *Language myths* (pp. 66–76). New York: Penguin.

Morakinyo, A. O. (1995). *Discourse variations in low income African-American and European-American kindergartners' literacy-related play*. Unpublished doctoral dissertation, UMBC, Baltimore.

Morgan, C. (2006). What does social semiotics have to offer mathematics education research? *Educational Studies in Mathematics, 61*(1), 219–245.

Morgan, M. (2002). *Language, discourse and power in African American culture.* Cambridge, UK: Cambridge University Press.

Morris, E. (2007). "Ladies" or "loudies"?: Perceptions and experiences of black girls in classrooms. *Youth & Society, 38*(4), 490–515.

Morrison, F. J., & Connor, C. M. (2009). The transition to school: Child-instruction transactions in learning to read. In A. Sameroff (Ed.), *The transactional model of development* (pp. 183–201). Washington, DC: American Psychological Association.

Morrison, T. (1993). Nobel lecture. *The Nobel Foundation.* Retrieved August 4, 2009, from http://nobelprize.org/nobel_prizes/literature/laureates/1993/morrison-lecture.html

Mos Def. (1999). Love. On *Black on both sides* [Audio CD]. New York: Rawkus.

Mos Def. (2004). Magnificent. On *The dangerous mix* [Audio CD]. No label.

National Center for Education Statistics. (2009). The nation's report card (National Assessment of Educational Progress). Retrieved October 31, 2009, from http://nces.ed.gov/nationsreportcard/

National Council of Teachers of English & International Reading Association. (1996). *Standards for the English language arts.* Urbana, IL, and Newark, DE: National Council of Teachers of English and International Reading Association.

Nelly. (2002). Hot in herre. On *Nellyville* [Audio CD]. New York: Umvd.

Nowicki, S., & Carton, J. (1993). The measurement of emotional intensity from facial expressions. *Journal of Social Psychology, 133*(5), 749–750.

Nunberg, G. (2002). A loss for words. Retrieved August 4, 2009, from http://people.ischool.berkeley.edu/~nunberg/vocabulary.html

Oakes, J. (1987). Tracking in secondary schools: A contextual perspective. *Educational Psychologist, 22*(2), 129–153.

Odell, L., Vacca, R., & Hobbs, R. (2007). *Elements of language: Fifth course* (teacher's edition). Austin, TX: Holt Rinehart and Winston.

Odell, L., Vacca, R., Hobbs, R., & Irvin, J. L. (2001). *Elements of language: Introductory course* (annotated teacher's edition). Austin: Holt, Rinehart, and Winston.

Odlin, T. (1989). *Language transfer: Cross-linguistic influence in language learning.* Cambridge, UK: Cambridge University Press.

Ogbu, J. U. (2003). *Black American students in an affluent suburb: A study of academic disengagement.* Mahwah, NJ: Erlbaum.

Oliver, M. L., & Shapiro, T. M. (1995). *Black wealth/White wealth: A new perspective on racial inequality.* New York: Routledge.

Paris, D. (2009). "They're in my culture, they speak the same way": African American language in multiethnic high schools. *Harvard Educational Review, 79*(3), 428–447.

Paul Laurence Dunbar homepage. (2003). Retrieved August 1, 2009, from http://www.dunbarsite.org/

Persell, C. H. (2007). Social class and equity. In J. A. Banks & C. A. M. Banks (Eds.), *Multicultural education* (6th ed.). Hoboken, NJ: John Wiley & Sons.

Peterson, S. S., & Kennedy, K. (2006). Sixth-grade teachers' written comments on student writing: Genre and gender influences. *Written Communication, 23*(1), 36–62.

Piestrup, A. M. (1973). *Black dialect interference and accommodation of reading instruction in first grade* (Monographs of the Language-Behavior Research Laboratory). Berkeley: University of California.

Popham, J. (2001, April 25). Interview: James Popham. Retrieved from http://www.pbs.org/wgbh/pages/frontline/shows/schools/interviews/popham.html

Poplack, S., Van Herk, G., & Harvie, D. (2002). "Deformed in the dialects": An alternative history of non-standard English. In P. Trudgill & R. Watts (Eds.), *Alternative histories of English* (pp. 87–110). London: Routledge.

Prentice Hall writing and grammar: Communication in action: Silver level. (2003). (handbook.). Upper Saddle River, NJ: Pearson Prentice Hall.

Preston, D. (1998). They speak really bad English down South and in New York City. In L. Bauer & P. Trudgill (Eds.), *Language myths* (pp. 103–112). New York: Penguin Books.

Purcell-Gates, V. (1997). *Other people's words: The cycle of low literacy.* Cambridge, MA: Harvard University Press.

Ravesteijn, W., de Graaff, E., & Kroesen, O. (2006). Engineering the future: The social necessity of communicative engineers. *European Journal of Engineering Education, 31*(1), 63–71.

Redd, T. M., & Webb, K. S. (2005). *A teacher's introduction to African American English: What a writing teacher should know.* Urbana, IL: National Council of Teachers of English.

Reed, J. S. (1982). *One South: An ethnic approach to regional culture.* Baton Rouge: Louisiana State University Press.

Reed, J. S. (1992). *Whistling Dixie: Dispatches from the South.* Orlando: Harvest Books.

Reed, J. S. (1993). *My tears spoiled my aim: And other reflections on Southern culture.* New York: Harcourt.

Reed, J. S., & Reed, D. V. (1996). *1001 things everyone should know about the South.* New York: Doubleday.

Reid, D. K., & Valle, J. W. (2004). The discursive practice of learning disability: Implications for instruction and parent school relations. *Journal of Learning Disabilities, 37*(6), 466–481.

Richardson, E. (2003). Race, class(es), gender, and age: The making of knowledge about language diversity. In G. Smitherman & V. Villanueva (Eds.), *Language diversity in the classroom: From intention to practice* (pp. 40–66). Carbondale: Southern Illinois University Press.

Rickford, J. R. (1999). *African American Vernacular English: Features, evolution, educational implications.* Malden, MA: Blackwell.

Rodriguez, J. I., Cargile, A. C., & Rich, M. D. (2004). Reactions to African-American Vernacular English: Do more phonological features matter? *Western Journal of Black Studies, 28*(3), 407–414.

Romaine, S. (1994). *Language in society: An introduction to sociolinguistics.* Oxford, UK: Oxford University Press.

Roscigno, V. J. (1998). Race and the reproduction of educational disadvantage. *Social Forces, 76*(3), 1033–1061.

Rudes, B. A. (2004). Multilingualism in the South: A Carolinas case study. In M. Bender (Ed.), *Linguistic diversity in the South: Changing codes, practices, and ideology* (pp. 37–48). Athens: University of Georgia Press.

Salatino, A. J. (1995, January). *Will Appalachia finally overcome poverty?* Kuttawa, KY: McClanahan.

Salmons, J., Jacewicz, E., & Fox, R. A. (2008, January). *Fast talkers vs. slow talkers: Speech rate across dialect, generation and gender.* Paper presented at the American Dialect Society, Chicago.

Salvia, J., Ysseldyke, J., & Bolt, S. (2006). *Assessment: In special and inclusive education* (10th ed.). Florence, KY: Wadsworth.

Scarborough, H. S., Charity, A. H., & Griffin, D. (2003, June). *Linguistic challenges for young readers.* Paper presented at the Society for the Scientific Study of Reading, Boulder, CO.

Schiffrin, D. (1984). Jewish argument as sociability. *Language in Society, 13*(3), 311–335.

Schiffrin, D. (1994). *Approaches to discourse.* Oxford, UK: Blackwell.

Schleppegrell, M. J. (2001). Linguistic features of the language of schooling. *Linguistics and Education, 12*(4), 431–459.

Schleppegrell, M. J. (2007). The linguistic challenges of mathematics teaching and learning: A research review. *Reading & Writing Quarterly, 23*(2), 139–159.

Scott, J. C., Straker, D. Y., & Katz, L. (Eds.). (2008). *Affirming students' right to their own language: Bridging language policies and pedagogical practices.* New York: Routledge and the National Council of Teachers of English.

Serpell, R., Baker, L., & Sonnenschein, S. (2005). *Becoming literate in the city: The Baltimore early childhood project.* New York: Cambridge University Press.

Serrie, J. (2002, October 23). Country DJ too Southern for station. Retrieved July 30, 2009, from http://www.foxnews.com/story/0,2933,66422,00.html

Seymour, H. N., Roeper, T. W., & de Villiers, J. (2003). *Diagnostic evaluation of language variation—screening test (DELV screening test).* Upper Saddle River, NJ: Pearson.

Shadyac, T. (Director). (2003). *Bruce almighty* [Film]. New York: Universal Studios.

Shelton, N. R., Altwerger, B., & Jordan, N. (2009). Does DIBELS put reading first? *Literacy Research and Instruction, 48*(2), 137–148.

Smalls, I. (2004). *Don't say ain't.* Watertown, MA: Charlesbridge.

Smith, M. W., & Wilhelm, J. D. (2007). *Getting it right: Fresh approaches to teaching grammar, usage, and correctness.* New York: Scholastic.

Smitherman, G. (1986). *Talkin and testifyin: The language of Black America.* Detroit: Wayne State University Press.

Smitherman, G. (2000). *Talkin that talk: Language, culture, and education in African America.* London: Routledge.

Smitherman, G., & Villanueva, V. (Eds.). (2003). *Language diversity in the classroom: From intention to practice.* Carbondale: Southern Illinois University Press.

Smitherman-Donaldson, G. (1987). Toward a national public policy on language. *College English, 49*(1), 29–36.

Snow, C. E., Burns, S., & Griffin, P. (Eds.). (1998). *Preventing reading difficulties in young children.* Washington, DC: National Academy Press.

Soukup, B. (2000). *"Y'all come back now, y'hear!?": Language attitudes in the United States towards Southern American English.* Unpublished master's thesis, University of Vienna, Vienna, Austria.

Steele, C. M. (1992). Race and the schooling of Black Americans. *Atlantic Monthly, 269*(4), 68–78.

Steele, C. M., & Aronson, J. (1995). Stereotype vulnerability and the intellectual test performance of African Americans. *Journal of Personality and Social Psychology, 69,* 797–811.

Stockman, I. J. (1996). Phonological development and disorders in African American children. In A. G. Kamhi, K. E. Pollock, & J. L. Harris (Eds.), *Communication development and disorders in African American children: Research, assessment, and intervention* (pp. 117–153). Baltimore, MD: Brookes.

Stockman, I. J. (2000). The new Peabody Picture Vocabulary Test–III: An illusion of unbiased assessment? *Language, Speech, and Hearing Services in Schools, 31*(4), 340–353.

Stover, L., & NCTE Standing Committee on Teacher Preparation and Certification. (2006). Guidelines for the preparation of teachers of English language arts. Retrieved November 3, 2009, from http://www1.ncte.org/store/books/middle/126639.htm

Strauss, S. (2005). *Positioning yoga: Balancing acts across cultures.* New York: Berg.

Strunk, W., & White, E. B. (2000). *The elements of style* (4th ed.). Boston: Allyn & Bacon.

Suitts, S. (2007). A new majority: Low-income students in the South's public schools. Retrieved July 29, 2009, from http://www.sefatl.org/pdf/A%20New%20Majority%20Report-Final.pdf

Tarone, E. E. (1973). Aspects of intonation in Black English. *American Speech, 48*(1/2), 29–39.

Tatum, B. D. (2003). *"Why are all the Black kids sitting together in the cafeteria?": And other conversations about race.* New York: Basic Books.

Terrell, S. L., & Terrell, F. (1983). Effects of speaking Black English upon employment opportunities. *Journal of the American Speech and Hearing Association, 25*(6), 27–29.

Terry, J. M., Evangelou, E., & Smith, R. L. (2009). *Dialect switching and mathematical reasoning tests: Implications for early educational achievement.* Unpublished manuscript.

Terry, N. P. (2008). Addressing African American English in early literacy assessment and instruction. *Perspectives on Communication Disorders and Sciences in Culturally and Linguistically Diverse Populations, 15*(2), 54–61.

Tillery, J., Wikle, T., & Bailey, G. (2000). The nationalization of a Southernism. *Journal of English Linguistics, 28*(3), 280–294.

Toepke, A., & Serrano, A. (Directors). (1998). *The language you cry in: Story of a Mende song* [Film]. San Francisco: California Newsreel.

Tucker, G. R., & Lambert, W. E. (1969). White and Negro listeners' reactions to various American English dialects. *Social Forces, 47,* 463–468.

Turner, L. D. (1949). *Africanisms in the Gullah dialect.* Chicago: University of Chicago Press.

University of North Carolina at Chapel Hill (UNC-CH), Center for Teaching and Learning. (1997). *Teaching for inclusion: Diversity in the college classroom.* University of North Carolina. Retrieved July 29, 2009, from http://cfe.unc.edu/pdfs/TeachforInclusion.pdf

University of Oregon Center on Teaching and Learning. (n.d.). DIBELS letter naming fluency. Retrieved August 7, 2009, from https://dibels.uoregon.edu/measures/lnf.php

Urban dictionary homepage. (2009). Retrieved August 1, 2009, from http://www.urbandictionary.com/

U.S. Census Bureau. (2006, December 22). Press release: Louisiana loses population; Arizona edges Nevada as fastest-growing state. Retrieved October 29, 2009, from http://www.census.gov/Press-Release/www/releases/archives/population/007910.html

U.S. Census Bureau. (2008, August 14). Press release: An older and more diverse nation by midcentury. Retrieved July 28, 2009, from http://www.census.gov/Press-Release/www/releases/archives/population/012496.html

Vanneman, A., Hamilton, L., Anderson, J. B., & Rahman, T. (2009). *Achievement gaps: How Black and White students in public schools perform in mathematics and reading on the National Assessment of Educational Progress* (No. NCES 2009-455). Washington, DC: National Center for Education Statistics, Institute of Education Sciences, U.S. Department of Education.

Virginia Department of Education. (n.d.). *Virginia Standards of Learning.* Retrieved August 1, 2009, from http://www.doe.virginia.gov/go/Sols/home.shtml

Wallace, D. F. (2001, April). Tense present: Democracy, English, and the wars over usage. *Harper's Magazine, 302*(1811), 39–58.

Washington, J. A. (1996). Issues in assessing the language abilities of African American children. In A. G. Kamhi, K. E. Pollock, & J. L. Harris (Eds.), *Communication development and disorders in African American children: Research, assessment, and intervention* (pp. 35–54). Baltimore, MD: Brookes.

Washington, J. A., & Craig, H. K. (1992). Performances of low-income, African American preschool and kindergarten children on the Peabody Picture Vocabulary Test–Revised. *Language, Speech, and Hearing Services in Schools, 23*(4), 329–333.

Whiteman, M. F. (1981). Dialect influence in writing. In M. F. Whiteman (Ed.), *Variation in writing: Functional and linguistic cultural differences* (pp. 153–166). Hillsdale, NJ: Erlbaum.

Wickham, D. (2005, June 6). Southern migration fuels gains for Blacks. *USA Today.* Retrieved July 29, 2009, from http://www.usatoday.com/news/opinion/columnist/wickham/2005-06-06-wickham_x.htm

Wilder, M. (2000). Increasing African American teachers' presence in American schools: Voices of students who care. *Urban Education, 35*(2), 205–220.

Wilkinson, C. (1999). On being "country": One Affrilachian woman's return. In D. Billings, G. Norman, & K. Ledford (Eds.), *Back talk from Appalachia* (pp. 184–186). Lexington: University of Kentucky Press.

Wolfram, W. (1994). The phonology of a socio-cultural variety: The case of African American Vernacular English. In J. Bernthal & N. Bankson (Eds.), *Child phonology: Characteristics, assessment, and intervention with special populations* (pp. 227–244). New York: Thieme Medical Publishers.

Wolfram, W. (1998). Black children are verbally deprived. In L. Bauer & P. Trudgill (Eds.), *Language myths* (pp. 103–112). New York: Penguin.

Wolfram, W. (2000). Everyone has an accent. *Teaching Tolerance Magazine, 18*(23), 18–23.

Wolfram, W. (2006). Why do American Southerners talk that way? In E. M. Rickerson & B. Hilton (Eds.), *The five-minute linguist: Bite-sized essays on language and languages* (pp. 116–119). Oakville, CT: Equinox.

Wolfram, W., Adger, C. T., & Christian, D. (2007). *Dialects in schools and communities* (2nd ed.). Mahwah, NJ: Erlbaum.

Wolfram, W., & Thomas, E. R. (2002). *The development of African American English.* Oxford, UK: Blackwell.

Wolfson, N., & Manes, J. (1980). Don't dear me! In S. McConnell-Ginet, R. Borker, & N. Furman (Eds.), *Women and language in literature and society* (pp. 79–92). New York: Praeger.

Wurr, A. J., & Hellebrandt, J. (2007). *Learning the language of global citizenship: Service-learning in applied linguistics.* Bolton, MA: Anker.

Wyatt, T. A., & Seymour, H. N. (1999). Assessing the speech and language skills in preschool children. In E. V. Nuttall, I. Romero, & J. Kalesnik (Eds.), *Assessing and screening preschoolers: Psychological and educational dimensions* (pp. 218–239). Boston: Allyn & Bacon.

Young, R. (2008, April 12). High profile: Joe Rice; Folksy, relaxed local lawyer "at the top of his game." *The Post and Courier.* Retrieved May 30, 2010, from http://www.postandcourier.com/news/2008/apr/12/joe_rice36841/?print

About the Authors

ANNE HARPER CHARITY HUDLEY is Assistant Professor of English, Linguistics, and Africana Studies and the inaugural William & Mary Professor of Community Studies at the College of William & Mary in Williamsburg, Virginia. Her research and publications address the relationship between English language variation and K–16 educational practices and policies. Charity Hudley has served as a consultant to the National Research Council Committee on Language and Education and to the National Science Foundation's Committee on Broadening Participation in the Science, Technology, Engineering, and Mathematics (STEM) sciences. She is on the editorial board of the sociolinguistics division of *Language and Linguistics Compass* and on the Linguistic Society of America Committee on Linguistics in Higher Education as an undergraduate program representative and head of diversity initiatives. She has worked with K–12 educators through lectures and workshops sponsored by the American Federation of Teachers and by public and independent schools throughout the United States.

Dr. Charity Hudley earned both a B.A. and an M.A. in linguistics from Harvard University in 1998. She was awarded a Ford Pre-Dissertation Fellowship in 2003. From 2003 to 2005, she was the Thurgood Marshall Dissertation Fellow at Dartmouth College. She earned a Ph.D. in Linguistics from the University of Pennsylvania in 2005. She received a National Science Foundation Minority Postdoctoral Fellowship in the fall of 2005 and a National Science Foundation Minority Research Starter Grant in 2009.

CHRISTINE MALLINSON is Assistant Professor in the Language, Literacy, and Culture Program and Affiliate Assistant Professor in the Gender and Women's Studies Program at the University of Maryland, Baltimore County (UMBC) in Baltimore, Maryland. Her research investigates the social contexts of English language variation, particularly with regard to region, ethnicity, social class, and gender. She has conducted extensive field research in Appalachia and throughout North Carolina, as well as in Washington, D.C., and Baltimore, Maryland. Mallinson is the associate editor of *American Speech*, managing and developing the annual Teaching American Speech pedagogical section, and she moderates the TeachLing online discussion group on linguistic pedagogy. She also serves on the editorial board of the sociolinguistics division of *Language and Linguistics Compass* and is a member of the executive committee of the Southeastern Conference on Linguistics.

Dr. Mallinson received a B.A. in sociology and German from the University of North Carolina at Chapel Hill in 2000 and an M.A. in English with a concentration in sociolinguistics from North Carolina State University in 2002. She received the Nancy G. Pollock Graduate School dissertation award for the College of Humanities and Social Sciences at North Carolina State University, where she earned a Ph.D. in Sociology and Anthropology, with concentrations in sociolinguistics and social inequality, in 2006.

Index